LABOR 'TIL DELIVERANCE

Beverly Barnes Brown

Copyright © 2020 by Beverly Barnes Brown

All rights reserved. No part of this publication may be reproduced by any means, graphics, electronic, or mechanical, including photocopying, recording, taping, or by any information storage retrieval system without the written permission of the publisher except in the case of brief quotations embodied in critical articles and reviews.

Beverly Barnes Brown/Rejoice Essential Publishing
PO BOX 512
Effingham, SC 29541

www.republishing.org

Unless otherwise indicated, scripture is taken from the King James Version.

Scripture quotations marked (NIV) are taken from the Holy Bible, New International Version®, NIV®. Copyright © 1973, 1978, 1984, 2011 by Biblica, Inc.™ Used by permission of Zondervan. All rights reserved worldwide. www.zondervan.com The "NIV" and "New International Version" are trademarks registered in the United States Patent and Trademark Office by Biblica, Inc.™

All Scripture quotations are taken from THE MESSAGE, copyright © 1993, 2002, 2018 by Eugene H. Peterson. Used by permission of NavPress. All rights reserved. Represented by Tyndale House Publishers, a Division of Tyndale House Ministries.

Scripture quotations marked (ESV) are taken from The Holy Bible, English Standard Version® (ESV®) Copyright © 2001 by Crossway, a publishing ministry of Good News Publishers. All rights reserved.

Labor 'Til Deliverance/ Beverly Barnes Brown

ISBN-13: 978-1-946756-93-0

Library of Congress Control Number: 2020902521

DEDICATION

This book is dedicated to the glory of God.

TABLE OF CONTENTS

FOREWORD..ix

INTRODUCTION..1

CHAPTER 1:   Onset of Labor...5

CHAPTER 2:   Free, yet Labor Continues..........................10

CHAPTER 3:   The Episiotomy
               The Cutting Away...18

CHAPTER 4:   Babe In Christ,
               Spiritual Midwife Needed............................34

CHAPTER 5:   The Test...40

CHAPTER 6:   The Breach..65

CHAPTER 7:   Another Push..93

CHAPTER 8:   Led Into A Desert Place
               For Deliverance..116

CHAPTER 9:   Summary...139

ABOUT THE AUTHOR..149

FOREWORD

I am beyond excited to write the foreword for my mother's new book on deliverance. Growing up, I can distinctly remember my mother praying for others in the church. I am not talking about saying a few words, but fervently praying for God's people hours on end. She would pray for the young people during the camp meeting services. She would help cast out demons and demonic spirits from the people of God, all through the power of the blood of Jesus. My mother truly has a heart to see the people of God healed, delivered, and set free. For God did not give us the spirit of bondage, but the spirit of adoption, whereby we cry, Abba, Father (Romans 8:15).

My mother realizes that helping people attain their full deliverance is hard work. In a sense, it is like labor. Think about it for a second. Prior to giving birth, a woman often undergoes hours of labor. She may have to endure painful contractions to prepare the baby for its arrival into the world. Just as labor is a rigorous process that leads to a miracle, deliverance is a rigorous process that leads to freedom.

My mother understands that while deliverance is greatly needed, deliverance ministries are lacking in the body of Christ. They go to church every Sunday with problems and leave with those same problems. For instance, people go to church with anxiety, depression, suicidal thoughts, shame, and guilt only to leave bound by the same strongholds. My mother understands that Jesus came to give life and that more abundantly. But sometimes, we must usher people (and ourselves) through deliverance in order to achieve that abundant life.

In this book, my mother gives a detailed account of her journey of deliverance. She uses the wisdom that God has given her to help others obtain their deliverance as well. If you have been struggling with an issue for years, *Labor 'til Deliverance* will provide you with the tools you need to be delivered. If you are a prayer warrior, this paperback will challenge you to pray fervently for your fellow man. If you are a church leader, this book will inspire you to make deliverance a mainstay in the church. Let us put a spotlight on deliverance, for this is the will of God.

—Merlendi Brown, LVN, RN, BSN, FNP student

BIOGRAPHY

MERLENDI BROWN holds a Bachelor of Arts in Psychology, Bachelor of Science in Nursing, and will soon have a Master of Science in Nursing. She works as a registered nurse in the Dallas area. Not only does Merlendi understand and care for the physical and mental needs of her patients, but she also understands the importance of spiritual deliverance. She is a prayer warrior, child of God, and an avid supporter of the *Labor 'til Deliverance* book.

INTRODUCTION

LABOR 'TIL DELIVERANCE

Spiritual deliverance does not come easy, nor does it come cheap. There is a spiritual price to pay. Deliverance is often birth through much toiling, laboring, and pushing in a spiritual sense. Deliverance is a process by which God rescues His people from bondage, from troubles, or from the snares of the enemy, which is Satan. There is a divine purpose and a God-given destiny for every believer. Many of us may experience many trials, adversities, and difficulties on the road to our destiny. We must labor in prayer, study, and obey God's Word to overcome our adversary, the devil, and get to a place of deliverance. After deliverance from one trial, there may be a short rest, but until the day of Jesus Christ, there will always be other trials.

"Be sober, be vigilant; because your adversary the devil, as a roaring lion, walketh about, seeking whom he may devour:" — 1 Peter 5:8

That lets us know that the enemy will never leave us in peace. He comes to steal, kill, and destroy. However, not all trials are from the enemy; there are times when God will allow believers to go through fiery ordeals, and to suffer persecution. These situations are to help us as God's people, and they are for our good. When we are tested, it teaches us endurance, and bring us to the place where God is trying to get us to. God may even test us so that we may get to know Him better or to help us grow in Him. None of us like to be tested, but it is a part of being a Christian.

Labor 'til Deliverance highlights many struggles, trials, and tribulations that can be thought of as spiritual labor pains that eventually leads to deliverance. These may come in any form. Some trials come to reveal our character to teach us patience and to bless us. Some circumstances we find ourselves in may be because of our sins or transgressions, while others may be inflicted upon us by others, but then again, it may be that God is testing us. Either way, we must endure as good soldiers if we are committed to living a life pleasing unto God. We may have had a difficult childhood that caused us mental and/or physical pain. Some of us may have gotten side-tracked from our destiny by abusing drugs and alcohol. Others may have endured mental and physical domestic abuse, while some may have been dominated and abused by a spiritual leader or leaders. Another struggle is with falling back into sin after giving our lives to God. Then again, some of us have experienced demonic attacks, then gained authority after being delivered. Nevertheless, before receiving deliverance from demonic attacks, we must wage in spiritual warfare. We must fight in the spirit when we are in a spiritual battle.

For the weapons of our warfare are not carnal, but mighty through God to the pulling down of strong holds; — 2 Corinthians 10:4

The fight is not against flesh and blood. We are not warring against abusive parents, husbands, nor spiritual leaders. Of course, those people must be held accountable for their actions, but the actual enemy is an evil spirit working through these people to torment God's children. These evil spirits will try and cause them to miscarry their destinies.

> For we wrestle not against flesh and blood, but against principalities, against powers, against the rulers of the darkness of this world, against spiritual wickedness in high places. — Ephesians 6:12

For this reason, it is necessary to pray for spiritual discernment and be filled with the Holy Ghost to fight against the demonic realm in the name of Jesus. Many are the afflictions of the righteous, but the Lord delivers us out of them all. These spiritual labor pains (battles) may sometimes cause us to grow weary and stop fighting. They can also cause us to lose faith and stop trusting God to bring liberation. But then if we stop pushing and stop trusting God, the process of deliverance will be hindered or delayed. It is the enemy's job to try and block this process by trying to cause a spiritual abortion before our destiny is birth out. We, as children of God, must push in the spirit, travail in prayer, keep the faith, and trust the Lord to bring deliverance in every situation in our lives. Without total deliverance, we will walk around in bondage and darkness for years.

In natural childbirth, sometimes a C-section is needed to deliver the child. In the spiritual realm, for deliverance to be achieved, some people and some things must be (cut away) removed from our lives. For instance, if controlling parents try to continue the control, even after the child is grown and on their own, that relationship may need to be re-examined. Another example, we will need to distance ourselves from old friends with whom we once abused drugs. Lastly, if an abusive spouse refuses to get help, and they continue to abuse the other, then the marriage needs to be dissolved.

If allowed, these three examples may continue. By not getting fully delivered from demonic attacks, we ultimately are leaving a demonic door open for the enemy resulting in us remaining in bondage and darkness. Demonic doors opened through drug abuse, domestic abuse, spiritual abuse, and many other sins will require more than repentance. Soul ties need to be broken and those doors must be closed through spiritual deliverance.

After every deliverance comes peace and joy as we gain more strength and authority, learn patience and perseverance, and birth to a higher realm in God. Subsequently, everything that a child of God goes through will work for the good and the Lord will be glorified.

CHAPTER ONE

ONSET OF LABOR

After being given to my maternal grandmother at two weeks of age, she raised me for the most part. She loved me the best she knew how. She called me "Lady," and I was her pride and joy. Being in her care is the most positive thing that I recall with some shade of happiness from my childhood. With the help of God, she taught me, without intentionally teaching me about life. Mama Sugar, my grandmother, wasn't a religious person and only went to church on occasion. But God used her to show me goodness, how to be good to others, and how to persevere through the hard times. She didn't teach me much about spirituality, but she taught me about life. She taught by example. My grandmother was poor, handicapped, and could not read or write but didn't complain. I know it was God working through her and imparting into me compassion, love, caring for others, unselfishness, and perseverance. I have never known a kinder, humbler person than my Mama Sugar, who lived to be 94 years of age.

After I was school age, I had more contact with my birth mother, but my grandmother's house was where I encounter the most love and peace. I credit my grandmother with raising me because that's where I slept at night and where I spent most of my time. I cared for my birth mother who recently deceased, even though we did not have a close and loving I am the middle child and only girl. I felt as if I was a burden. Due to my gender, the possibility of getting pregnant was kept before me. My mother did not hide the fact <u>that she did not want children, but if she had children, she preferred boys</u>. That confession left me feeling as though I was a burden or a liability. I did not realize at the time, but this was also an open door for the spirit of rejection. My two brothers were seemingly preferred over me by my mother. I was a daddy's girl. My father and I got along a lot better than my mother and me. My childhood was strict, stifled, smothering, and went by too slow; it seemed never-ending. I remember longing for the day when I'd be an adult and could be on my own. I would have run away, but I didn't have the nerves. I was too afraid of the 'unknown' out there. So, I just spent many days 'wishing' I was never born. I had a longing to be grown and away from my mother. For me, that day could not come quick enough. We weren't allowed to have other children over to play. That time in my life was depressing. I spent more days being unhappy than I did being happy.

I was raised in church even though I spent my nights with Mama Sugar. Since she didn't go to church regularly, I went to my birth mother's house on Sunday mornings. She sent us to Sunday school, and she took us to church. From an early age, I always knew about God. I always heard the Word of God preached with fire. I knew that there is a 'heaven' and a 'hell.' Those old Baptist preachers preached that if we 'live right,' heaven will be our home. Their preaching always seemed to paint a vivid picture. When they preached about heaven, in my child's mind, I could almost see those streets paved with gold. I imagined the glory of God lighting up all of heaven, as the Word of God teaches in the Book of Revelation. This is the vision that God took the Apostle John up and showed him.

Revelation 21:21,23 says, 21"And the twelve gates were twelve pearls; every several gates was of one pearl: and the street of the city was pure gold, as it were transparent glass." 23"And the city had no need of the sun, neither of the moon, to shine in it: for the glory of God did lighten it, and the Lamb is the light thereof".

Heaven seemed like such a wonderful place. But on the other extreme, the preachers also taught and painted a picture of 'hell fire and brimstone' for the ones that don't 'live right' and that do not accept Christ as their personal Savior. The people whose names were not written in the book of life would burn in hell forever.

And if anyone's name was not found written in the book of life, he was thrown into the lake of fire. — Revelation 20:15 (ESV)

And if your eye causes you to sin, tear it out. It is better for you to enter the kingdom of God with one eye than with two eyes to be thrown into hell, where their worm does not die, and the fire is not quenched. — Mark 9:47-48 (ESV)

Even with hearing the Word of God preached every Sunday, still, I only knew 'about God,' but I didn't 'know God.' I believed God is real. There was something that seemed to fascinate me about "God." But God is calling for a relationship with Him, not a fascination. An intimate relationship with God, not through the pastor or our fore-parents that knew Him is what the Lord desires. I didn't know a lot about prayer. I just knew we should pray. We never prayed in the home, but I remember the deacons praying at church. I began praying before I went to bed. "Now lay me down to sleep, I pray the Lord my soul to keep, if I should die before I wake, I pray the Lord my soul to take." I somehow felt that would get me through until I decided to 'turn my life around' and accept Christ as my personal Savior.

School was an escape from home life, yet it was not an enjoyable experience for me. I was not allowed to participate in any school activities. When I reached Jr. High, I was ashamed to go to school every day because of the way my mother forced me to dress, and the way she made me wear my hair. After school, there was chores and homework. On weekends, there were chores, homework, and church. I could not invite friends over to visit. My two brothers were my playmates. I knew I was smart. I had the potential to do well, but I didn't apply myself. I only studied enough to pass. I just wanted to hurry, get grown, and get 'away' from home.

My birth mother had to have surgery when I was a senior in high school, and she demanded that I come live with her. So now, my nights and my days were spent under her roof. I missed my grandmother. My grandmother was very hurt that I had been taken away from her. Life got even harder because my mother and I didn't get along. There was a lot of fussing and arguing between my mother and my father. The home was not a peaceful one. I remember wishing I was never born. I lived in fear of doing or saying something wrong that would lead to a beating. The way my brothers and I were whipped was nothing short of abuse. Not that a child is not to be chastised, but there is a right way.

"He that spareth his rod hateth his son: but he that loveth him chasteneth him betimes." — Proverbs 13:24

But the way we were whipped went above and beyond the normal expected chastisement. We did not get spanked with switches but received beatings with the thick extension cords used to wire up a building. We got beatings with fan belts that are used on vehicles. The method my parents used to whip my brothers and I was cruel. Placed prostrate on the bed, my older brother holding one side of my body down and in one place, while my mother or father held the other side of my body, and the other parent would whip me until they felt I had enough. Depending on what I was being whipped for, there may have been a 'part 2' to the whipping.

I lived in constant fear of being whipped. Fear of beatings if the grades were not to my parents' satisfaction, fear of someone telling my parents something about me that they felt warranted a whipping. These beatings caused me to become bitter and full of anger. I felt helpless and it seemed that my only out was to run away, but I did not have the nerve. My baby brother did run away, but I just decided to wait for 'time' to bring about a change.

I graduated high school at 17 years of age. It was my father's wish that I would go to college and I wanted to go, but I could not stand the turmoil any longer. The strained (to say the least) relationship between my mother and myself by now had escalated. Even after my graduation, she still wanted to control my life. After a very heated disagreement between us, I walk out. I was grown and working. Therefore, the best option was to leave. At the time, I don't know if I loved my mother or not. I knew I didn't like her very well. I want to stress that I never raised my hand to my mother. I never thought about getting violent with her. I decided to leave and go back to my grandmother, and so I did. I told my dad I was leaving. He tried to talk me into staying so I could go to college. Daddy said, "Just ignore her. You know how your mother is." But I told him, "Daddy, I can't stay." I left walking down the highway back to my grandmother's house. I cared about hurting my dad by not going to college, but I had been in emotional pain and hurting for too many years. The emotional abuse, as well as physical abuse, had to end. The best option was that I removed myself from the situation. **It is always best to walk away, even if it means never looking back then to stay, and things escalate into physical violence between two adults or anyone.**

CHAPTER TWO

FREE, YET LABOR CONTINUES

I graduated high school at 17. I had never been on, not even one date. I never went to a high school prom or participated in any sports. My life growing up was not fun. With such a strict upbringing, I wanted to experience what I had been missing out on most of my entire life thus far. So, I hit the streets hard and heavy. With this new-found freedom upon leaving my parent's home, I rebelled and began to make terrible choices in my life. I became sexually active, even promiscuous, without even knowing I was on a destructive path. I hung out with the wrong crowd and got involved with a gentleman that had issues with a former girlfriend. The girlfriend and I got into an altercation. She stabbed me in the neck with an ice pick. I rushed to the emergency room. Getting involved in the wrong relationship was the first consequence of the bad choice that I had made. Thanks, be to God, I survived the attack. I did not know at the time of the attack that Isaiah 54:17 says:

"No weapon that is formed against thee shall prosper; and every tongue that shall rise against thee in judgment thou shalt condemn. This is the heritage of the servants of the LORD, and their righteousness is of me, saith the LORD."

I was introduced to drugs, marijuana, specifically. I began to drink beer and enjoyed getting high because it seemed to fill a void that I desperately needed filled. I smoked weed almost every day. I worked as a cook at a fast food job to support myself. I went out to the club every weekend. I smoked, danced, partied, got high, and had unprotected sex. I was having a good time, so I thought. I was heading down a destructive path that I knew I didn't belong on, nor did I desire to travel. But I kept going. I had a few lady friends, but they were on the same path as me. I was not surrounded by people to influence me in pursuing better choices in life. Mama Suga was the only positive voice that I had in my life, but I didn't listen. I had been denied freedom too long, and I did not want to deprive myself of the little happiness that I felt when I was getting high and partying.

B. REPEATING THE CYCLE (BONDAGE LIKE GROWING UP)

Again, I begin dating a gentleman that was also involved with another woman. I put myself in danger by dating him because the woman was very violent. I never had any confrontation with her directly, but she confronted him with a pistol. Thankfully, no one was injured. This guy began to abuse me physically. He was very strong and I was a petite teenager. I was no match for him. Therefore, I couldn't defend myself against him. I kept dating him, even with the abuse. While riding with this boyfriend and his friend, I was attacked again by him. This time his friend came to my rescue. The friend started fighting my boyfriend at the time because he was trying to tell him that I was too little to beat on. I thought that was very chivalrous. I started to like the friend that stopped me from getting abused by my then boyfriend. The friend began to like me. I broke up with the boyfriend that was abusing me at that time and I began to date 'my protector.' Little did I know that he would become the 'master abuser.' This new boyfriend and I got along good for about two months. We thought we were in love. He was married at the time, but he was separated from his then wife. I had nothing to do with their separation. He and I began to live together. He was a heavy drinker and I was a heavy dope smoker. It seemed to work for a couple of months.

After the newness wore off our relationship, he began to exhibit his true character. He began to abuse me in every way possible, physically, emotionally, and sexually. It was the beginning of what would become the worst time of my life. I had left the physical and emotional abuse (never any sexual abuse as a child) that I had to endure as a child growing up. The freedom from the abuse I had just came out of as a child growing up, only lasted a few short months. I had allowed myself to become chained and bound again. I say 'allowed' because I had a choice in this situation. As a child, the only option I felt I had was to endure until I became an adult. Now being an adult, unknowingly, I choose abuse rather than walking away. But this man was so abusive, walking away was not something that he would allow. He was very jealous, abusive, controlling, and dominating. I felt like a child all over again, because he treated me like his. He treated me as his property, only worse than one would expect. He abused me in the name of love. Afterward, he would cry and say, "I'm sorry. I love you. It won't happen again." I soon found out that it was a seemingly never-ending cycle.

The beatings were usually triggered by his excessive drinking. He was such the jealous type that I wasn't allowed to talk to any men other than my brothers. As a matter of fact, this man was even jealous of my brothers. My brothers and I were close. One of my brothers was close to my boyfriend, but the way this boyfriend really felt about my relationship with my brothers came out after the boyfriend got drunk. He was jealous of my brothers and accused us of sleeping together. I never told my brothers the truth, because I was ashamed of the things this man said and the things he did to me. I didn't know what I had gotten myself into, but he made it clear that he wasn't letting me out of the relationship alive. I even tried to leave him quite a few times, but he would find me and force me to come back to him. I felt I had to return to him to keep the family members safe that I was staying with after I left him. I was his property to do with as he saw fit. I went back to him. I endured chokings and being hit in the face as well as other places. I was threatened with shotguns and knives. This man threatened to kill himself and me. There were times when I didn't' think I would make it out of this relationship alive. But God had angels protecting me even when I couldn't protect myself. I didn't know at that time that God had angels assigned to my life. Psalm 91:11 says:

"For he shall give his angels charge over thee, to keep thee in all thy ways."

At the time, all I knew to do was cry. I cried for many days and nights. Crying was my only outlet. But the crying seemed to turn him on even more. After the abuse and crying, he would want to have sex. He would force himself on me. Even if I fought, there was more abuse to follow. It was a very dark time, which appeared to be a hopeless situation. I suffered this abuse in silence. I lived in constant fear of saying or doing something that would trigger his rage. I didn't want anyone to know about the abuse, so I hid it. I was too ashamed and embarrassed to tell anyone. This man was so jealous, violent, deranged that if he was confronted with any opposition, he would hurt, remove anyone or anything thing that stood up against him. I had one brother that did not condone abuse, and he would have fought for me, had I told him. But that may have had cost him harm or cost his life at the hand of this man. I decided to keep silent. It was the only thing to do.

This man seemed to have a 'need' to treat me this way. It seemed to give him great joy to abuse and inflict harm on me. He was only good when he was sober. Even so, whatever he thought in his mind while he was sober, would manifest that when the drinking began, I would get abused for things that happened or what he thought occurred. He went to work during the week. He was a hard worker and he took care of the financial part of the relationship. I was not allowed to work. He usually did not drink heavily during the week while he worked. But I knew the pattern. From Friday to Sunday night, was a living hell. But, somewhere way off in my distant mind, I would tell myself, "I'm going to get out of this one day." I didn't know how. I never wanted to kill him, but it was just a 'knowing' that I would one day be free of him.

After we had been together for several months, I became pregnant. I was happy about the pregnancy because it was planned. With being pregnant, one would think the abuse would stop. It didn't. My child's father abused me even during my pregnancy. It was hard being happy about having my child and so sad at the same time about the abuse. I made it through the pregnancy. I gave birth to a beautiful baby girl. It was a happy time, getting to know my baby, but a sad time being in this relationship with this abuser. I just took one day at a time. I kept putting one foot in front of the other every day. I was going through the motions of being happy with this man. I kept trying to please him so as not to be abused. All this time, this dude and I were just living together. He asked me to marry him and I did. The marriage did not change anything other than my last name. The abuse continued.

In my unhappiness, in my enduring all this abuse, I found an avenue of relief. I had found a way to 'pay him back' for the abuse. I knew I was married, and it was against my beliefs, but I began an affair with my husband's friend. The affair did not make me happy, but it gave me revenge.

I didn't know at the time what the Bible says about revenge: "Dearly beloved, avenge not yourselves, but rather give place unto wrath: for it is written, Vengeance is mine; I will repay, saith the Lord." — Romans 12:19

The affair went on for a little while. I don't think my husband ever knew about it. Because had he known, it probably would have meant the loss of lives. After the affair ended, I didn't have any other options that would bring me revenge for the abuse I endured. My weariness of the whole relationship increased. I had fallen out of love with my then husband years ago. All the beatings and the abuse had taken all feelings away for him. After 6 ½ years, I knew there was nothing left but to get out of this marriage. I can't say I wasn't afraid of him any longer. I guess I was tired of caring. Somewhere along the course of the years, I had acquired the nerves to make some moves to free myself from this marriage. I decided that I could not and would not accept the abuse any longer. The first thing I did was get a job. I had to have funds to take care of my daughter and myself without him. He was against me working, but by this time, I didn't care. I was beyond caring. I had to find some peace of mind, and the only way to have peace was to leave him.

I kept working for a few months on a job I didn't like, but I was determined to support my daughter as best I could. I slowly began to stay away from home, even when I was not working. My then husband and I worked different shifts, so that worked very well in my favor. He began to see that something had changed in me. He sensed that I didn't care anymore. The abuse was not as frequent, but it was too late. In my mind, I was on my way out the door. He tried to treat me better, but there was no use. My mind was made up. I was leaving.

All the years I had been with him, I endured so much abuse that a dog did not even deserve. He threatened to kill me on many occasions. But the last beating I received at his hands was so traumatic. I had left him, and I think he knew that I had no intention of coming back to him. He followed me to a concert in Houston, Texas. He found me at a relative's house. He 'kidnapped' me and forced me to go outside with him to the vehicle. I had no choice but to go with him. He proceeded to beat me until I told him where the vehicle I had been driving was. He threw me on the ground and stood over me with a screwdriver. Then he proceeded to stab me in the middle of my chest with it. The only reason I lived from that attack was nothing short of God's hand of mercy. God, Himself, showed me mercy once again. Of all the people standing around looking at the attack, not one person lifted a finger to help. But God's mercy stood in the gap.

> Isaiah 59:19 (The Message Bible)
> [15-19] GOD looked and saw evil looming on the horizon—
>   so much evil and no sign of Justice.
> He couldn't believe what he saw:
>   not a soul around to correct this awful situation.
> So he did it himself, took on the work of Salvation,
>   fueled by his own Righteousness.
> He dressed in Righteousness, put it on like a suit of armor,
>   with Salvation on his head like a helmet,
> Put on Judgment like an overcoat,
>   and threw a cloak of Passion across his shoulders.
> He'll make everyone pay for what they've done:
>   fury for his foes, just deserts for his enemies.
>   Even the far-off islands will get paid off in full.
> In the west they'll fear the name of GOD,
>   in the east they'll fear the glory of GOD,
> For he'll arrive like a river in flood stage,
>   whipped to a torrent by the wind of GOD.

I thank God that I lived through the attack. I escaped him by running across the street to the police station for help. That was the last attack that I suffered at his hands. After that encounter, I was more determined than ever, never to go back to him. I don't know if he felt he had lost control of me, or if he had found someone else. I didn't care at this point. He didn't hunt me and force me to come back to him. Maybe he had found someone else. If he had any affairs, I never knew about them. I left the apartment, clothes, furniture, and everything. I only wanted my baby from the relationship. It was a difficult time, even after I left him. I had no family support. My family didn't want to keep my daughter while I worked because they wanted me to go back to the marriage. But I had made my choice and it would not have had made sense for me to go back. I suffered through not having any family support. I kept working and got an apartment for myself and my daughter. Things got easier as time went on.

CHAPTER THREE

THE EPISIOTOMY
THE CUTTING AWAY

I embarked upon a new life as a single parent. Looking back, I know God was there every step of the way. I decided then and there that I would never allow myself to be treated that way ever again. I admit I was ashamed that the marriage didn't work out. I felt I had failed. Only God and I know the pain and agony I suffered in that marriage. The marriage was destined to fail, given the variables from the beginning. I accepted that failure, and I learned from my mistakes. I admit I carried bitterness for a long time. It seemed life had not treated me fair. First, I was bound in my childhood issues, then bound by a very abusive husband.

After the breakup, my daughter's father was still active in her life. She spent most weekends with him and his new girlfriend. I focused on raising my daughter and moving forward. I continued smoking marijuana. I partied off and on. By now, being exposed to a different set of acquaintances, I was offered stronger drugs, IV drugs, but since I knew that I'm a leader not a follower by nature, I said no. I got involved with guys that sold dope. Therefore, I began to sell it as well. When selling drugs, one is introduced to people from all walks of life. I got involved with a dude that was into using and selling different types of drugs. I helped him sell by making drops and doing pick-ups when he asked. I managed to stay out of the police way for a while. Then they came and kicked my door in looking for drugs. Thankful to God, I was not arrested and no drugs were there at the time. I made bad decisions and I continued to sell drugs.

By the mid to late 80's, crack cocaine had hit the streets. I began by only selling crack. Then, somehow, I wanted to experiment and smoke it. I didn't like the crack pipe, but I crushed the rock cocaine and smoked it in my marijuana. It has the same similar addictive effect, either smoking by pipe or in weed. I would smoke, but I could never get enough. I was ashamed of myself, but I yet smoked. I was rapidly losing weight. I tried to accommodate my appearance by wearing baggy clothing, trying to hide the fact that I had lost so much weight. When smoking crack, I could seemingly feel myself losing weight. I could feel the weight falling off my bones. I didn't know at that time that drugs are a demonic spirit, *pharmakeia*.

I was being taken on a trip. I was going down another destructive path. I had made it out of my childhood woes with my mother and a very abusive marriage, yet here I was sentencing myself to another type of jail. I found myself in bondage all over again, just a different jail cell. I could not recognize myself when I looked in the mirror. But I could not stop smoking. Even after all the crack was gone and I didn't have money to buy more, I would find myself crawling around on the floor, looking for a little crumb to get just one more hit. I was on a journey that could have taken me to an even darker place, to jail, or I could have died. I remember smoking so much crack that my heart fluttered and ran away beating so fast. I would only stop long enough to catch my breath. Then I would fire up another joint of crack cocaine. I kept telling myself that I was going to stop smoking, but I would not follow through.

During this season of my life, I only had one daughter. She was with her grandparents and her dad a lot, so she was safe from the unsavory people that this life brings around. She was always fed, clothed, and protected. You see, when God has a plan for your life, His mercy and grace will only allow us so much space and time while we partake in destructive behavior.

"For I know the thoughts that I think toward you, saith the LORD, thoughts of peace, and not of evil, to give you an expected end." — Jeremiah 29:11

I wasn't privy to this knowledge at the time. But looking back, I know it was only God that I'm still here. Even while partaking in the drugs, I always knew that this was not the life I wanted to lead. I knew deep down that I wanted so much more out of life. I wanted to be somebody with respect and integrity. I wanted to go places in life, but most of all, I wanted to be a better mom to my daughter, and I wanted to be saved.

"For what shall it profit a man, if he shall gain the whole world, and lose his own soul?" — Mark 8:36

Through all my heartaches and trials, God has spared my life so many times. The life I was leading was dangerous because I took a lot of chances with my safety. I had people coming in the wee hour of the night to buy dope with me being in the house alone. I could have been killed, raped, or had terrible things happen to me. HIV and AIDS were at an all-time high. I was putting myself at risk by continuing to have unprotected sex. But God covered me. Thank you, Jesus.

The path I was on was very trying. It was taking me to a place that some people don't ever return. But I had enough understanding to know that even with the drugs, sex, and the life I was leading, I still was not happy. Given all the drugs I was using, I was never satisfied. I always had a longing and felt lonely. I remember getting on my knees and praying to God that He would turn me around before it was too late. You see, I remember what those old Baptist preachers had taught me in church. I knew God was there all the time. I remember the preacher saying that God would never leave us nor forsake us. I keep getting high, but I prayed.

I got pregnant again while still using drugs. This pregnancy was not planned. I didn't think I could conceive again. But to my surprise, I find myself pregnant once again. In all honesty, at first, I was not happy. I was alone, smoking dope, scared, was not in a good place in my life, and to bring a child into that life was not a good idea, I thought. I continued to smoke crack at the beginning of the pregnancy. In my warped way of thinking, I thought maybe the baby would not survive. I didn't know what else to do. Having an abortion was not an option. I was very much in need of a change in my life, but in my thinking, having another child was not the answer, or so I thought.

After a few weeks, I began to feel a change in my mind. I accepted the pregnancy and my unborn child. I woke up one day and stopped smoking all drugs. The Bible tells us in James 1:17 that every good gift and every perfect gift is from above. That lets me know that this change of heart concerning smoking dope and change of mind came from God above. I disassociated myself from anyone that was using any drugs. I got myself together, mentally and physically, by eating right and working out faithfully. I felt happy as I took care of myself and my unborn baby. My older daughter was a big help to me in the pregnancy. She pampered me and took good care of me. After I got myself together, I had a very good outlook on life. I began to enjoy being pregnant. This pregnancy was different from the first in that I was not getting abused this time around. My unborn baby's biological father was not around. I didn't have to live in fear because I was not in an abusive relationship or dating anyone. I enjoyed the pregnancy to the fullest. At the consummation of time, my second child, another beautiful baby girl, was born. She was to be spoiled from the very beginning by her big sister, as well as myself.

After bringing my baby girl home from the hospital, there was a calm, peace, and joy. My oldest daughter did everything for her. She was like a second mother to her baby sister. We were one big happy family, my two girls and myself. I had been clean and sober for months. I knew I would never smoke crack again, but for whatever reason, I decided to smoke marijuana on occasion. All drugs are bad and should never be touched. However, I talked myself into smoking only marijuana. Also, I started selling drugs again to help support myself and my girls. Selling drugs was quick money, but there was always the threat of being busted by the police. There were people all around the apartment complex, where I lived getting arrested and sentenced to prison for selling drugs. I saw where children were getting taken away from their parents and put into CPS custody, and I knew that this was not an option for my children. It was my responsibility to raise my children. Therefore, I chose to stop selling drugs permanently. And I did, but I continued to smoke weed. The police were not as bad on a person for smoking weed as they were selling crack. But I knew then, and I know now that it was the grace of God that kept me from ever getting arrested and subsequently sent to prison. I know it wasn't my smarts in maneuvering and staying off the police radar. It was God.

I resumed my old habit of smoking marijuana after my baby was born because there was still a void inside that I was trying to fill with the drugs. I knew I needed to get out of the life of drugs. I owed it to my girls and to myself to do things the right way. Also, I had this urging inside, telling me I needed to change my way of life. I was tired of my life the way I had been living it. My two girls were the only two good things that I had going for me. I kept telling myself that I was going to stop smoking weed, but every deadline I gave myself to quit, came and went with no success. I did not know at the time, but it was God that was calling me to a place in Him. I desired to quit smoking and do the right things, but I didn't have the power within myself to do that. I sensed that God was saying that my time out in the world was up and I was to give myself to Him entirely. I thought that I would stop sinning and smoking weed, then I would give my life to Christ. I never could stop of my own strength. But Christ didn't come to give His life for us because we were righteous, but to make us righteous through Him.

"But God commendeth his love toward us, in that, while we were yet sinners, Christ died for us." — Romans 5:8

That lets me know that I didn't have to get everything right before I came to Him, I needed to come to Him just as I was.

[28] Come unto me, all ye that labour and are heavy laden, and I will give you rest.
[29] Take my yoke upon you, and learn of me; for I am meek and lowly in heart: and ye shall find rest unto your souls.
[30] For my yoke is easy, and my burden is light. — Matthew 11:28-30

I knew God was calling me, but I was resisting and fighting. I didn't want to give up the life I was living. I didn't have many friends. I was only close to my two daughters. Even though I was not entirely happy, I felt that to live for God was too much of a sacrifice. I didn't have any peace. Frustrated, I continued smoking weed. I went swimming on the beach one weekend, partying and smoking marijuana. After I returned home, I noticed some rashes on my arms that were itchy and very bothersome. I was afraid to go to the doctor, for fear that it was a deadly disease, maybe AIDS. Since it was the early 90's,

AIDS was a huge scare, especially if someone was having or had been having unprotected sex, such as myself. I started to entertain the possibility that I had AIDS. I did not have a lot of knowledge about the disease but knew enough to know that most people don't live a long full life with it. In addition to the rashes, I had some sensations going on in my jaws.

I had concluded that unless I give my life to Christ, I may not live long enough to see my girls grow up. I knew enough to know that God saves, heals, delivers, and sets the captives free. I felt my only option was to give my life to Christ and let Him heal me. My imagination was working overtime. I could not rest, day or night. I kept my fears to myself. I did not have a blood test done. Since I had been having unprotected sex for years, and to increase the risk of maybe having contracted the disease, I had unprotected sex with IV drug users. So, I feared I most likely had the disease.

I was very anxious and fearful for the next few weeks. I knew that whatever the outcome of what was going on in my body was a very pivotal time. I was in a position that I had to make some hard choices. I only had one option, get into God's face and let Him heal me. I did not know exactly how to make that happen, other than just asking Him to come into my life. Given everything that I had experienced in my life from a stressful childhood to an even more stressful marriage and what I felt I might be facing, I needed something drastic to happen in my life.

While riding with a cousin, looking for some weed and beer to help mellow me out, and take my mind off my situation for a minute, I saw a big tent being built in a small town close to my home. I asked what was going on over there. My cousin told me that the people were getting it ready for a revival that was to begin the following week. I thought that was very interesting. I had never been to a tent revival meeting. I had grown up going to church. Even in my adult life, I had gone to church from time to time. But going under a tent for a revival was foreign to me. I knew of the evangelist that was conducting the revival. He was a prophet. I didn't exactly know what a prophet does, but I had heard that they prophesied and 'saw stuff' that was to happen in the future. Even though I was afraid of being called out, prophesied to, and the future being foretold, I felt an unction to go to one of the meetings. I agreed to go with my cousin to the revival the next week. At that moment, we drank our beer and smoked our weed. I felt that this was the last joint of marijuana that I would ever smoke, and likely the last drink of beer that I would feel the need to drink to fill the emptiness in my soul.

On the following week, the night came that we were to go to the tent revival meeting. I was apprehensive, but there was no turning. I had a 'feeling of knowing' that this was what I was supposed to do. I got dressed, and my cousin and I went to the meeting. We sat through the service. We watched as people sang, danced, shouted, spoke in a language that we could not understand, and praised God. I was accustomed to a different side of church service than this meeting. I was used to the choir singing, a sermon preached, and a few people jumping, shouting, and crying. But this worship service was something different. Not strange, but different. It was explained to us that it was the Holy Ghost that was moving in the service that caused the people to run when no one was chasing them. It was the Holy Ghost that caused the people to speak in a language that we had not heard a lot about. This was a Holy Ghost revival meeting. The sound of the worship service was different for me. It was electrifying. I somehow connected and drawn to this sound.

[2] And suddenly there came a sound from heaven as of a rushing mighty wind, and it filled all the house where they were sitting.

³ And there appeared unto them cloven tongues like as of fire, and it sat upon each of them.

⁴ And they were all filled with the Holy Ghost, and began to speak with other tongues, as the Spirit gave them utterance. — Acts 2:2-4

My cousin and I sat, looked, and observed. I found that I was not afraid anymore of this type of atmosphere. I was in awe and I just went with the flow. Of course, I was called out by the prophet and given a prophetic word. I sensed a new beginning on the horizon for me. Originally, I had planned to go to the meeting only one night. But after the first night, I felt compelled to go back the next night, and the entire week. On the last night of the revival meeting, I experienced the Holy Ghost first hand. I had found that in revival meetings, they also did something that the saints called 'tarrying'. Tarrying is where those that are really seeking God, the things of God, and a mighty move of God in their life go to the altar. At the altar, they get on their knees, clap their hands, pray and cry out to God for as long as necessary. They pray and cry out until the Holy Ghost comes in and takes control. There are some prayer warriors there to help pray with the seekers. Prayer warriors are some of the members of the church that has a calling to pray and intercede for others. They are there to help the seekers 'pray through.' They labor with the seekers in prayer until the Holy Ghost comes in. The prayer warriors should have a grace to labor with the souls that are seeking God until the Holy Ghost comes upon the one seeking.

I felt something drawing me to the altar. I found myself getting up and walking down the aisle towards it. I was seeking 'something' but I didn't know exactly what to do after I got there, I just knew that I had to have a change in my life. I would soon find that this was the catapult that I needed to push me to the place I needed to go. Once I made it to the altar, I got down on my knees. I was asked a few questions to let the prophet know what it was that I sought after. He had preached on the baptism of the Holy Ghost that night. In his sermon, he had expressed what the Holy Ghost is and what He does in a person's life. The Holy Ghost is the third person to the Godhead. There is the Father, who is God. There is the Son, which is Jesus. There is the Holy Ghost, that combined with the Father and the Son, they are One. He preached that when a person wants Christ to come in their life, they first need to repent of their sins, accept what Jesus did on Calvary, be baptized, then they need to be filled with the Holy Ghost.

Then Peter said unto them, Repent, and be baptized every one of you in the name of Jesus Christ for the remission of sins, and ye shall receive the gift of the Holy Ghost. — Acts 2:38

But ye shall receive power, after that the Holy Ghost is come upon you: — Acts 1:8

In his sermon, he talked about how that when the Holy Ghost comes in, it changes a person and makes things new, by leading, guiding, comforting, and a host of other things. At the altar, I thought yes, I need the Holy Ghost. I became repentant. I asked God to forgive me for every sin that I had ever committed. I told God that I accepted His son Jesus. I told Jesus that I need Him and everything He had to give me. I then asked Him to fill me with the Holy Ghost. I begin to look around at the others to get some indication of what to do next, and how I should do it. The prayer warrior that was assigned to 'pray me through' told me I should get on my knees, close my eyes, and get my mind directly on Jesus. I followed her directions. The seekers at the altar begin to pray and cry out to God. It seemed that quite a length of time had passed as I prayed and cried out of my soul. I was desperate, tenacious, broken, and had nowhere else to turn. I had tried everything else and it had failed me. I had nowhere else to turn but to God. And He was right there with His mighty outstretched hand.

After I had been on my knees for what seemed like a very long time, I was asked to stand. I received assistance before I could stand on my own. I continued to clap my hands and cry out to God. After a few minutes, I felt 'something' which was not coming for without but coming from within. I noticed I had no control of my body. I loosen up and let go. The power of the Holy Ghost took over my entire being. I really can't describe it. One will have to experience it. I just gave in and let God have His way. I had never felt this way before, the joy, peace, and calmness. I had experienced some with being off and on drugs for almost 18 years and not one of those highs could compare to what God was doing with and within me at that moment.

I arrived there with my hair in a nice hair style and wore a little short dress. I thought I was looking cute, but after that encounter with the Holy Spirit, my hair was drenched, my clothes were dirty, and I did not care. God had purged me from deep down inside my belly. I felt so good afterward that I had control of my body again. I felt light and free. In my entire life, I had never felt like this before. I knew I was a changed woman, different, and God had set me free. I would never use street drugs ever again. At that moment, what I had been running from led me to an experience that will stay with me forever. I left that tent that night on a high that can only come from above. It only came from God. Out of all the street drugs I had used, I never felt satiated or that I had had enough. But after this encounter with the Holy Ghost, I felt filled, but I still wanted and needed more, but differently than with the drugs.

Matthew 5:6 says, "Blessed are they which do hunger and thirst after righteousness: for they shall be filled." I found that we, as children of God, should have a constant hunger/thirst for Him and the things of the Kingdom. God is sovereign and has no limitations. Therefore, He fills us by leaving us hungry and thirsty at the same time. We are blessed to keep this yearning for God until the day of Jesus Christ.

I went home that night with a new mind and a new determination. I was a new person because I felt joy and peace that I had never felt before. I used to hear the saints quote the Scripture, "The joy of the Lord is your strength." Now I knew what they meant. I had found the Lord found joy. What I had been missing all my life, I had received that night. I wanted to tell everyone about my salvation. I had accepted Christ as my personal Savior. I did not just repeat after the preacher and shake the preacher's hand. I had an encounter with God almighty. At the altar, I was contrite. I repented of my sins. I purposed in my heart to live holy and follow Christ with all my might. I was truly changed.

I told some family members about my salvation and my experience with the Holy Spirit. They didn't believe that I had changed overnight. Also, they were skeptical about the Holy Ghost. They probably had never had an experience with the Holy Ghost. It is sad to know that some people go to church every Sunday for years and never had an encounter with God. I found that it's 'good religion' to go to church every Sunday, even if we never experience the glory of God. But I also found that 'good religion' will not get us into heaven. We must have an intimate relationship with God. Yes, we need to attend church as Hebrews 10:25 says, "Not forsaking the assembling of ourselves together," but that alone is not sufficient in itself for salvation. We must strive daily for that intimate relationship with God. We need to become more like Him every day. We need the Holy Spirit to give us power and to keep us daily. We need to be a witness to God's saving power. There is a dying world out there and without God's power, we can't effectively witness and draw others to Christ.

Acts 1:8 says, "But ye shall receive power, after that the Holy Ghost is come upon you: and ye shall be witnesses unto me both in

Jerusalem, and in all Judaea, and in Samaria, and unto the uttermost part of the earth."

I did not let the negativity of what others thought about my new Christian walk phase me. I had been born again. Therefore, I was determined to hold on to God's unchanging hand. What others thought, even the negativity from my family, didn't matter to me in the least, they did not die for me. Christ gave his life for me and I owe Him my life. The only one I needed to or will ever need to please is God. I only need to live a life that's pleasing to God, not man.

Proverbs 16:7 says, "When a man's ways please the LORD, he maketh even his enemies to be at peace with him."

I felt different, changed, and thought differently. For the first time that I can remember, I had peace. I had a peace of mind, something that I can't remember having during my childhood, and definitely not during the marriage. My family, as well as my friends, looked and treated me differently. They were not my concern. This new life was something I had been searching for years. I lost more than a few friends, and some family members were alienated, but I knew I was on the right track and nothing and no one was going to turn me around. Wow, I am now born again. I am a new creature in Christ Jesus.

2 Corinthians 5:17 says, " Therefore, if anyone is in Christ, he is a new creation; old things have passed away; behold, all things have become new."

I didn't need to worry about changing things in my life. My newfound love for God directed where I went, who I associated with, and how I conducted myself daily. I no longer had a desire for drugs or to go to the clubs. A friend told me that I need not try to run the race in one day, but to pace myself and take one day at a time. I found that when we come to know and accept this loving God, we wonder why we resisted so long. We feel sorrowful and may even think that we need to make it up to God for not accepting Him before now. We cannot make up or go back to yesterday. We can only go forward and purpose in our hearts to do all within our power to please God and rely on the Holy Spirit to strengthen us day by day.

Paul tells us in Philippians 3:13-14, "Brethren, I count not myself to have apprehended: but this one thing I do, forgetting those things which are behind, and reaching forth unto those things which are before, 14 I press toward the mark for the prize of the high calling of God in Christ Jesus."

I have found that when we have gone through so many trials and tribulations in life, more times than not, we have a great call on our lives. I don't believe that God allows us to go through things just for the sake of going through them. As a matter of fact, in Romans, we find that whatever we go through, it's working together for our good. Nothing we go through will be wasted.

I found that it is easier to forgive those who have mistreated, abused, despitefully misused, and wronged us in any way in life. Just remember that all the pain they may have inflicted upon us is working for our good. In our carnal thinking, we may never be able to understand that concept, but Romans 8:28 tells us, "And we know that all things work together for good to them that love God, to them who are the called according to his purpose." That lets me know that whatever God allows, He has a purpose and a plan that is far greater than what the enemy intended when we were transgressed. As we grow in God and understand this Scripture, we may even go back and thank our oppressors, because the oppression was only setting the stage for greatness in our lives. But we learn from our mistakes. As we grow closer to God, by praying, fasting, reading His word, seeking Him, we become more like Him, and God is love.

"For God so loved the world that He gave his only begotten son, that whosoever believeth in him should not perish, but have everlasting life." — John 3:16

I began reading my Bible, something that I had never done, other than reading a few Scriptures occasionally when things got tough. I went to church on Sundays and weekly services. I found myself praying more and praying with understanding. I felt the peace of God in my daily walk with Him. I no longer had a desire for drinking, partying, fornicating, doing drugs, selling drugs, or any of the things that I did to pass the time or to make ends meet. Even though these are not the only sins, these were some that keep me from excepting Christ years before. Letting these things go was not a struggle for me. I did not have to fight not to smoke a joint. I no longer had the desire to get high and had no withdrawal symptoms. My new-found love for God superseded the passion for the things of the world. I know that it was not of my own strength that I had completely turned my back on my old life. I know it was God that was leading and guiding me day by day.

I feel that even after one becomes saved and gives their life to the Lord, if there's someone that we have wronged in the past before we accepted Christ, it is our responsibility to make amends with them. Case in point, one day, at a laundry mat, I cross paths with a woman that I had been having an affair with her husband before I was saved. She somehow knew about the affair and was very upset with me. I felt led to talk to her that day and ask her to forgive me for what I had done. She reluctantly forgave me. The Bible tells us in Matthew 5:23-24 [23] Therefore if thou bring thy gift to the altar, and there rememberest that thy brother hath ought against thee; [24] Leave there thy gift before the altar and go thy way; first be reconciled to thy brother, and then come and offer thy gift.

Whether she forgave me or not, I did what God required of me. Of course, we cannot go to every person that we may have sinned against to ask forgiveness. As God leads, we must try to make amends for our past transgressions as much as it is in our power to do so. That shows the love of Christ and humility when we humble ourselves and become repentant.

2 Corinthians 7:10 lets us know, "For godly sorrow worketh repentance to salvation not to be repented of:"

CHAPTER FOUR:

BABE IN CHRIST, SPIRITUAL MIDWIFE NEEDED

It is imperative that after we give our lives to God, we need the understanding to walk out our daily lives. It is so vital to read and study. We need the wisdom of God to make Godly decisions. As babes in Christ, we don't know exactly what God is expecting from us concerning some things that we may have been accustomed to doing. When we have that zeal for God, we don't want to sin against Him. Wise counsel is very important. A very godly and balanced spiritual mid-wife is needed to help in this stage of our new walk. Also, spiritual discernment is needed. But at this stage in my walk with God, I didn't even know there was a such thing as 'discernment.' I feel that this is one of the gifts that comes with time and experience walking with God. But at this stage, we can be very vulnerable and easily led or persuaded. It is easy to be led by tradition and by religion rather than by the Word of God.

Some Christians that had been saved and walking out salvation for a while, they meant well, but some of the teachings, beliefs, and instructions were not a commandment from God. Not that they taught against God, that was never the case, but some things that they called sin as I grew in Christ, I have come to understand that it was not sin. For instance, looking back, I now know that it is not a sin to trim my hair. A woman's hair is her glory. Therefore, God is expecting us to do what is needed to maintain good health and hygiene concerning our hair.

Some Christians feel that women of God should never trim their hair, or if they do, they are made to feel that they have sinned against God. Some of the more seasoned saints felt that we should not date or that our denomination should date of a certain denomination, which is not Biblical. How can we ever marry if we are not expected to date? It was taught that to marry someone from a different denomination was being 'unequaled yoke.' As far as denomination, I don't remember reading anything in the Word of God, stating that a specific denomination or group of people is more holy than the other. We all should be holy. There is no one set of people more saved or more holy than the other just because of denomination. When I gave my life to the Lord, there was a lot of controversy about a lady's dress code in the church that I attended, which caused a lot of confusion.

[9] In like manner also, that women adorn themselves in modest apparel, with shamefacedness and sobriety; not with braided hair, or gold, or pearls, or costly array;
[10] But (which becometh women professing godliness) with good works. — 1 Tim 2:9-10

In my experience as a new Christian, in my surroundings, more focus was put on the outward appearance than the inward appearance, the heart. When the heart is right, when we love God will all our heart, righteousness will flow out and it will be evident in everything we do, everything we say, in what we wear, even the places we go.

> Keep thy heart with all diligence; for out of it are the issues of life.
> — Proverbs 4:23

God is more concerned with our heart than if our dress is ankle length, or if we cross our legs a certain way in church. Of course, we need to dress modest, we need to sit respectfully, but I found that when we submit fully to God, let Him fill us with the Holy Ghost, He will do the leading and guiding in every area of our lives. In my new journey, after I became born again, I encountered a lot of different 'opinions' that caused a great deal of confusion in my mind. I started in a hurry, trying to do whatever I was told was right, and trying not to do what I was told a sin. I wore my dresses that reached my ankles. I wore stockings every day. I gave away a lot of my children's clothes that (as I grew in God) I discovered were perfectly acceptable and needed not to have been discarded. I was so confused at this stage and that confusion led to me doubting my salvation. I found that a lot of "do's and don'ts" were emphasized, rather than making sure my heart was pure, making sure I loved everyone, making sure I treated others with respect. The religious mindsets and religious traditions are hindrances to developing a healthy and intimate relationship with the true and living God and understanding by the Holy Ghost what God requires.

Of course, we need to represent Christ well in everything we do or say, but I found that if our heart is right, righteousness will flow out. With a lot of emphasis being put on religion, I made a lot of rash decisions concerning how I transitioned my children over into this new Christian walk. My oldest daughter was sixteen years of age and my baby daughter was almost four years of age when I gave my life to the Lord. The method of transition did not affect my baby daughter, as she was too young to understand the shift. But my oldest daughter was affected directly. A lot of things changed for her and regretfully, I did not give her a choice in the situation. At the time, I did not know how to orient her to the change that was happening in my life. In hindsight, I did not handle things well at all with her. I feel I caused her some embarrassment with her friends at school, because of the way I forced her to dress.

For example, I did not allow her to wear pants after my salvation. I gave all her pants and cute clothing away. She was only allowed to wear dresses and skirts. I did not explain things to her. I assumed that she should just obey. I did not consider her feelings. I did not sit her down and explain things to her in a way she could understand. With her being a very obedient child, she did not talk back or display any resistance to the changes that were being forced upon her. But not long after these demands and changes, she left to go live with her father until she finished high school. I didn't understand at the time, but I feel that I unintentionally pushed her away. I realized later, as I grew in Christ, that a lot of the demands and changes that I forced on her did not need to be made. As I grew up in my walk with God, I learned that the way I forced my girls to dress was because of tradition and religion. Religion looks at our outer appearance, but God looks at how our heart is dressed.

But the LORD said unto Samuel, Look not on his countenance, or on the height of his stature; because I have refused him: for the LORD seeth not as man seeth; for man looketh on the outward appearance, but the LORD looketh on the heart.— 1 Samuel 16:7

It can be very confusing if we are not diligent and get wise counsel. It is imperative to have guidance after we give our lives to the Lord. Whoever is leading and guiding us in the things of God, should be led by God and not by religion and traditions and not by their own opinions.

Wisdom is the principal thing; therefore, get wisdom: and with all thy getting get understanding. — Proverbs 4:7

As I grew in God, I realized the difference between a relationship with God and the traditional 'do's and don'ts' that may not be a requirement of salvation. As I grew in my relationship with God, I realized that I spent a lot of time working on my outward appearance rather than on the issues of my heart. I spent a lot of time trying to do 'what I was told' by others, thinking that was the way of salvation. I did not have, nor did I know I needed to pray for the discerning of spirits immediately after becoming a new Christian. I was not told that I needed to make sure I did not hold any unforgiveness against my ex-husband for all abuse that he had inflicted upon me. I was never told that I needed to forgive my birth mother and be delivered from my childhood upbringing. Even though I had no desire to relapse and start using drugs again, I was never told that I needed to make sure that I was completely delivered from drugs. I did not know that some doors had been open in the spirit realm due to my drug use, the spirit of *Pharmakei*, as well as other doors that needed to be closed in the spirit.

I was never told that I needed to be watchful so that the enemy would not try and re-enter in other ways. These are things of the heart that God I believe is more concerned with than He is with whether I wear stockings every day, whether I wear a pair of pants, or whether I marry a godly man from a different denomination than the one I am associated with. If I decide not to wear stockings every day, but I dress modest and I'm lifting up holy hands and have a pure heart, then God is pleased. I was bound to make mistakes. If I kept a repentant heart and a contrite spirit, then my God is well pleased even if I go against what man says just as long as I am obedient to God and to God's will.

Then Peter and the other apostles answered and said, We ought to obey God rather than men. — Acts 5:29

But the LORD said unto Samuel, Look not on his countenance, or on the height of his stature; because I have refused him: for the LORD seeth not as man seeth; for man looketh on the outward appearance, but the LORD looketh on the heart.— 1 Samuel 16:7

Though I am grateful for the prayers and some of the teachings in my early Christian walk, as I continue to grow in God, I realized that more teaching and training should have been put on the things of the heart, complete deliverance, and making sure the doors that had been open to the enemy was completely closed through deliverance. I feel as though those seasoned saints taught and trained what they knew at the time. I cannot deny that those saints of old played a large part in my Christian walk. They labored with me at the altar. They tarried with me for the Holy Ghost to come in. I am forever grateful, but now I know that from the background I came from, and because of the call on my life, I needed more intense ministry and deliverance. I needed the 'after care,' that goes with a person coming off drugs and promiscuity. I needed more focus to be put on the cleansing of my heart from old wounds, from scars left by being abused growing up and the domestic abuse that I suffered. I needed to be told what to be watchful for. As I have grown in God, I now know that I needed ministry to break all those soul ties with past sexual partners as well as ungodly soul ties to family members.

CHAPTER 5

THE TEST

Doors were left wide open and the enemy did RE-ENTER. I had given my life to Jesus, I had received the baptism of the Holy Ghost, but doors from my past were unknowingly left open and it was only a matter of time before the enemy would try and re-enter.

⁴⁴ Then he saith, I will return into my house from whence I came out; and when he is come, he findeth it empty, swept, and garnished.
⁴⁵ Then goeth he, and taketh with himself seven other spirits more wicked than himself, and they enter in and dwell there: and the last state of that man is worse than the first. Even so shall it be also unto this wicked generation. — Matthew 12:44-45

If the enemy can't get in one way, he will try another approach. Satan looks for a weak or a sore spot. He looks for a sore spot from an old hurt or old wounds that did not receive its complete deliverance and may be still festering. In the natural, without proper treatment, wounds can become infected and become susceptible to other microorganisms. This infection is likely to spread to other areas of the body. As it is in the spirit, without complete deliverance from past issues, the door is still open and other spirits can enter in. Certain issues or weaknesses may lay dormant for a while, even years, but eventually, without proper deliverance, those weaknesses can manifest and lead to a lifestyle displeasing to God. I was moving along very well, so I thought in my Christian journey. I was trying to do everything as right as I could. I was working in the church, busy doing things for God, and praying. I was not drinking or smoking. I felt my heart was delivered from unforgiveness. I was not committing adultery. I was trying my best to live holy and to be a good Christian. But just being good is not enough. The Word of God tells us we should be watchful unto prayer. Satan is strategic and he knew that I knew I was completely delivered from drugs. I did not doubt of my deliverance from drugs. So, he didn't try to tempt me with drugs. The strategy he used was loneliness, along with my sexual desires. I was not watching out for this attack. I had not been with a man sexually for quite a few years, ever since I was saved. In retrospect, the enemy had been plotting and scheming all along. He was waiting for that moment when I was at my weakest. He came with a great temptation gift wrapped in an enticing little box. But even at the weakest point in our Christian walk, when we are being tempted on every side, God always provides a way of escape. We must choose to take the way of escape that God provides.

There hath no temptation taken you but such as is common to man: but God is faithful, who will not suffer you to be tempted above that ye are able; but will with the temptation also make a way to escape, that ye may be able to bear it. — 1 Corinthians 10:13

To accept the route of escape that God provides, we have to deny ourselves.

Mark 8:34 says: "Whosoever will come after me, let him deny himself, and take up his cross, and follow me."

After we accept Christ, our lives are no longer ours. We belong to Christ. He purchased our lives when He gave His life on Calvary's cross. After then, we have a cross to bear. In bearing that cross, we must deny the flesh and the sinful desires of the flesh. The enemy was waiting before he made his move. He was waiting until I thought I had it all together. I was still sitting in church, singing in the choir, dancing, shouting and speaking in tongues, going through the motions of being strong in the Lord and the power of His might. I looked, acted, walked, and talked saved, but I was backsliding all at the same time. I did not realize it at the time, but doors had been left open to the enemy to re-enter. Ungodly soul ties had not been severed from my past. The spirit of lust had not been cast out when I got saved. Even though I walked right into the enemy's trap, I walked in with my eyes wide open. When temptation came, I chose not to use the way of escape that God provided repeatedly. I knew what I was about to do was so very wrong. I knew once I gave in to the enemy, I could not undo what I was about to do. Once we have sex with someone, we cannot turn around and un-sleep with them. Once sexual sin is committed, it forms new soul ties and strengthens old soul ties with the other person or persons. Not to mention that we are sleeping with everyone that person or those persons have slept with. Sure, we can receive forgiveness as long as the blood is running warm in our veins. But there is a price tag.

Romans 6:23 tells us that the wages of sin is death.

So, even though God will forgive, we still must give into account of all our deeds done. Also, sin separates us from true communion with God. Sin can cost us more than we are willing to pay. I promise I am not boasting, nor am I glorifying what I did, but I willfully sinned. It was pre-meditated. I continue to regret that terrible mistake that I knowingly made.

[26] For if we sin willfully after that we have received the knowledge of the truth, there remaineth no more sacrifice for sins,

²⁷ But a certain fearful looking for of judgment and fiery indignation, which shall devour the adversaries.

²⁸ He that despised Moses' law died without mercy under two or three witnesses:

²⁹ Of how much sorer punishment, suppose ye, shall he be thought worthy, who hath trodden underfoot the Son of God, and hath counted the blood of the covenant, wherewith he was sanctified, an unholy thing, and hath done despite unto the Spirit of grace?

³⁰ For we know him that hath said, Vengeance belongeth unto me, I will recompense, saith the Lord. And again, The Lord shall judge his people.

³¹ It is a fearful thing to fall into the hands of the living God. — Hebrews 10:26-31

For translation purposes of these KJV scriptures, the Message Bible version reads:

If we give up and turn our backs on all we've learned, all we've been given, all the truth we now know, we repudiate Christ's sacrifice and are left on our own to face the Judgment—and a mighty fierce judgment it will be! If the penalty for breaking the law of Moses is physical death, what do you think will happen if you turn on God's Son, spit on the sacrifice that made you whole, and insult this most gracious Spirit? This is no light matter. God has warned us that he'll hold us to account and make us pay. He was quite explicit: "Vengeance is mine, and I won't overlook a thing" and "God will judge his people." Nobody's getting by with anything, believe me. — Hebrews 10:26-31

So, I spat on the sacrifice that made me whole. I turned on God's Son. I insulted the spirit of God. God even let me know that if I consented to what the enemy was proposing, it would be one of the worst mistakes that I would regret it and it would cost me. It would not be just a one-time sin. It would be significant in a very negative way. I knew better and I could have said no. But my excuse to myself was that I was lonely, I was missing out on that very important part of life. I had strong sexual desires that were not being fulfilled. At the time, I was not strong enough nor delivered enough to run and hide in God. The doors of lust had never been closed years ago, so the enemy had legal right to enter back in with the spirit of lust. So, I yielded to temptation and committed adultery. It was not just a one-time sin. It was an on-going affair. And this affair would eventually lead to the next affair. Even though still in the church, I was backslidden. To backslide means to relapse, regress, weaken, give in to temptation, go astray, leave the straight and narrow. I had relapsed and weakened. I gave in to temptation. I was once close to God, but I allowed sin to steer me away from Him, yet calling myself saved and sanctified.

Really and truly, I was not being fulfilled sexually, even though I was having sex. The strongholds in my mind let me be satisfied with the idea of being with a man and having sex. I was deceived into being fascinated by the idea of a man wanting to be with me. I even began to watch pornography and masturbate, (which are both cardinal sins). I committed these 'extra' sins to compensate for the hollow feeling that I was left with after the unfulfilling sex I had engaged in. I learned from the past use of drugs that sometimes, the use of one drug leads to the use of another drug to enhance the first drug. Similar scenario, the sex was not satisfying physically, therefore to compensate, I felt the need to watch porn and masturbate, which lead to even more guilt and shame. Little did I know that I was opening even more doors and giving the enemy more legal grounds to have assess into my life.

Oh yes, every time I sinned, I would follow up with asking God to forgive me. Somewhere along the journey, I had learned from the things I had heard that if someone has a weakness such as lust, just keep repenting to God and ask forgiveness. However, my Bible tells me that I must humble myself, repent and then turn from the sin, then God will forgive and heal.

If my people, which are called by my name, shall humble themselves, and pray, and seek my face, and turn from their wicked ways; then will I hear from heaven, and will forgive their sin, and will heal their land.— 2 Chronicles 7:14

We know God is a gracious and forgiving God. He is just and faithful to forgive. We should not frustrate the Holy Ghost by continuing in sin. Yes, we make mistakes. Yes, we sometimes do wrong. No, we are not perfect, but if we do fall into sin, we should not continue in the sin. We should confess our sins to God. We should be honest with ourselves and with God, because He knows anyway. We should become repentant, become broken and contrite. He is waiting to forgive us. God already made provisions, because He knew we would sin. He had already sent His Son to die, and He died for any and every sin we would ever commit.

[1] What shall we say then? Shall we continue in sin, that grace may abound?
[2] God forbid. How shall we, that are dead to sin, live any longer therein? — Romans 6:1-2

If we confess our sins, he is faithful and just to forgive us our sins, and to cleanse us from all unrighteousness. — 1 John 1:9

My little children, these things write I unto you, that ye sin not. And if any man sin, we have an advocate with the Father, Jesus Christ the righteous:— 1 John 2:1

Once we yield to temptation and fall into sin, it cannot be undone. It can be forgiven, but it is on record in heaven and we will face judgment. Every sin we have ever committed has repercussions. God will judge. I have wished maybe a thousand times that I would have resisted the enemy and not yielded to the spirit of lust. It was by far one of the worst mistakes I have ever made. After I had fallen into sin, I had no peace and joy. I felt empty. Even though I kept going to church, I kept being faithful in church duties. I kept paying my tithes and giving offerings. I kept sacrificing doing things for God, but I was not obedient to God. Those things that I was doing for God were not acceptable to God. God wants total obedience.

And Samuel said, Hath the LORD as great delight in burnt offerings and sacrifices, as in obeying the voice of the LORD? Behold, to obey is better than sacrifice, and to hearken than the fat of rams. — 1 Samuel 15:22

To those looking from the outside, it appeared that I was living saved. I had good religion. But religion is not what God is calling for. God is calling for relationship. He requires intimacy with Him. He is looking for total commitment. Just good religion is not acceptable unto God. He commands us to live holy. God wants a complete Yes.

Because it is written, Be ye holy; for I am holy. — 1 Peter 1:16

I beseech you therefore, brethren, by the mercies of God, that ye present your bodies a living sacrifice, holy, acceptable unto God, which is your reasonable service. — Romans 12:1

All unrighteousness is sin, but sexual immorality is sin against the body. It's intertwined with the heart and soul and mind, as well as with the body. 1 Corinthians 6:18 reads that every other sin is outside the body, but the sexually immoral person sins against his own body.

⁹ Know ye not that the unrighteous shall not inherit the kingdom of God? Be not deceived: neither fornicators, nor idolaters, nor adulterers, nor effeminate, nor abusers of themselves with mankind,

¹⁵ Know ye not that your bodies are the members of Christ? shall I then take the members of Christ, and make them the members of an harlot? God forbid.

¹⁶ What? know ye not that he which is joined to an harlot is one body? for two, saith he, shall be one flesh.

¹⁷ But he that is joined unto the Lord is one spirit.

¹⁸ Flee fornication. Every sin that a man doeth is without the body; but he that committeth fornication sinneth against his own body.

¹⁹ What? know ye not that your body is the temple of the Holy Ghost which is in you, which ye have of God, and ye are not your own?

²⁰ For ye are bought with a price: therefore glorify God in your body, and in your spirit, which are God's.— 1 Corinthians 6:9, 15-20

1 Corinthians 6:15-20 (Message version)

God honored the master's body by raising it from the grave. He'll treat yours with the same resurrection power. Until that time, remember that your bodies are created with the same dignity as the master's body. You wouldn't take the master's body off to a whorehouse, would you? I should hope not.

There's more to sex than mere skin on skin. Sex is as much spiritual mystery as physical fact. As written in Scripture, "The two become one." Since we want to become spiritually one with the Master, we must not pursue the kind of sex that avoids commitment and intimacy, leaving us lonelier than ever—the kind of sex that can never "become one."

There is a sense in which sexual sins are different from all others. In sexual sin we violate the sacredness of our own bodies, these bodies that were made for God-given and God-modeled love, for "becoming one" with another. Or didn't you realize that your body is a sacred place, the place of the Holy Spirit? Don't you see that you can't live however you please, squandering what God paid such a high price for?

The physical part of you is not some piece of property belonging to the spiritual part of you. God owns the whole works. So let people see God in and through your body.

Sexual sin was more dangerous than I had originally thought. I thought that just merely asking forgiveness would suffice if I was truly repentant. I thought as long as I turned and stopped committing adultery, everything else would fall into place. I had no idea that soul ties were formed with the other person. I did not know these soul ties would have to be broken, which explains why every time I made up my mind to end the affair, I would find myself going back. This behavior continued far too long. Eventually, I gained enough strength to break off the affair completely. I successfully closed that chapter on that affair, but a few years later, since the spirit of lust and perversion had not been cast out, and the door was still open for the enemy, I found myself committing adultery again. Because the spirit of lust had never been cast out, it had the legal right and had built up strongholds. I had no idea how I could willingly allow myself to travel this sinful path all over again. It was like I was a different person, just going through the motions of being a child of God. I knew I had been gifted and called to be a prayer warrior.

When it came time to pray for others, I was too ashamed and felt condemned. I, myself needed prayer, I needed deliverance, but was too ashamed and did not know how to ask for it. I loved the ministry that I was associated with at that time, but not a lot of emphasis was not put on this type of sin. This type of hidden sin was swept under the rug. So, I hid from everyone the fact that I was involved in an adulterous relationship. It was not taught that if a person needed deliverance themselves, they should sit themselves down and get ministry. It was not taught that they should not lay hands on others until they were completely delivered and restored back in good standing with God.

I believe that the longer we disobey God and continue in sin, that's the more we become desensitized to His rebuke, and His voice. Sometimes we purposely shut out the voice of the Holy Spirit. God allows us free will. He wants us to choose to live for Him and choose to live holy. If we truly love God the way He desires us to, we will try hard and pray hard to not intentionally sin against Him. We will make mistakes, because we are not perfect, but we should make haste to repent and turn back to Him. Unrepentant sins in our lives dulls the voice of the Holy Spirit working in us. Unrepentant sins hinder the flow of the Holy Spirit through us, delays revival in each of us, and grieves the Holy Spirit.

Ephesians 4:30 tells us that we should not grieve the Holy Spirit.

The question may arise in one's mind, "How can a person that is saved and filled with the Holy Ghost fall in this type of continuous sin?" While yielding to sin can never be justified, I found that one reason, though not an excuse, could be as simple as the person may have gotten saved, but things were hidden, lying dormant, waiting on an opportune time to manifest itself. Another reason for some falling back into sin could be that they are void of understanding. We are in a wrestling match with demonic forces, and we are not matched for the devil in our own strength.

Submit yourselves therefore to God. Resist the devil, and he will flee from you. — James 4:7

For we wrestle not against flesh and blood, but against principalities, against powers, against the rulers of the darkness of this world, against spiritual wickedness in high places. — Ephesians 6:12

We must totally submit to God because He wants our whole heart. Some don't understand that we are in a life-or-death fight to the finish against the Devil and all his angels. For instance, when dealing with a spirit of lust, we cannot fight by carnal means and expect to win. We cannot just pray and hope for the best. We cannot just take a cold shower and go to bed. We cannot just lock ourselves away from those desires because the enemy has the legal right when the door is open because of the spirit of lust. The door is open because of ungodly soul ties to those past sexual partners that were never broken after the altar. Therefore, we must learn how to fight in the spirit.

For the weapons of our warfare are not carnal, but mighty through God to the pulling down of strong holds; — 2 Corinthians 10:4

2 Corinthians 10:3-6 The Message (MSG)

3-6 The world is unprincipled. It's dog-eat-dog out there! The world doesn't fight fair. But we don't live or fight our battles that way—never have and never will. The tools of our trade aren't for marketing or manipulation, but they are for demolishing that entire massively corrupt culture. We use our powerful God-tools for smashing warped philosophies, tearing down barriers erected against the truth of God, fitting every loose thought and emotion and impulse into the structure of life shaped by Christ. Our tools are ready at hand for clearing the ground of every obstruction and building lives of obedience into maturity.

We are no match for the devil in our own strength and with carnal weapons. These are strongmen and strongholds we are dealing with. The strongman is the spirit of lust, and the strongholds are adultery, fornication, masturbation, pornography, just to name a few. This battle can only be won with spiritual weapons. The church needs soldiers with training in spiritual warfare. The church should have mature Christians with spiritual discernment, that are well equipped to walk the babes in Christ through their deliverance. And not only the new converts, some seasoned saints still struggle with ungodly ties to their past life. The teaching and training should begin immediately after the person becomes saved and filled with the Holy Ghost. I say that because, when I gave my life to the Lord, I got saved and filled with the Holy Ghost, I got delivered from drugs, but the spirit of lust, fornication, adultery did not get cast out. All demons don't just leave after the altar. Those spirits were hidden and did not manifest until years later. I was void of understanding in this area. I had not been properly trained in warfare. Oh yes, I had given my life to Christ. I was not smoking marijuana anymore. I had stopped committing open sin, as the Lord gave me the grace and strength, but I found out through the things I suffered. There is so much more revelation needed as to not fall into repeated sin that leads to iniquities.

After the new converts tarry on the altar and receive Christ as their Lord and Savior, and get filled with the Holy Ghost, follow up with them so they won't fall back into continuous sin after salvation. One-on-one teaching sessions may be needed to address their lifestyle before accepting Christ. Spiritual discernment on the leaders and the prayer warriors' part is crucial. First, the leaders giving counsel, and the prayer warriors assigned to pray and walk these souls through deliverance, should be completely delivered and living holy as God gives them strength. Then, concerned, compassionate soldiers should talk to newly saved souls and find out what struggles they may have been struggling with before they gave their lives to the Lord. Teams of prayer warriors should have keen spiritual discernment, discreet, patience, and a heart of compassion. They should not be judgmental. The warriors should handle these souls with care, and with understanding because if it had not been for God, this could be their struggle. We were all sinners before we accepted Christ. We all needed deliverance from something, and some of us still need it. Therefore, we have no room to judge nor to be cynical.

Had I known that through drug use, adultery, feeling rejected and unwanted by my mother, there were open doors for the enemy to come in and set up strongholds, I would have been saved a lot of pain and heartache. Had I known that through me being a victim of domestic abuse that doors were opened for the enemy to have a legal right or have access to my life and lives of my children. Maybe if I had gotten completely delivered and closed all demonic open doors from my past, I might have been strong enough to fight when the enemy came to deceive me in fornication after I became a Christian. With my growth in God and learning about spiritual warfare, I realized that not only repentance was needed, but doors that gave the enemy legal right to bring some attacks and wage war against my children and me need to be closed. The enemy uses low points in our lives to mount an attack. He uses maybe when we are ill, resistance low, on drugs, been hurt, physically and emotionally. Also, the enemy will use our ignorance to mount an attack. Sometimes we don't get the teaching we need in some ministries to help us be watchful and prayerful. It is imperative that we are afforded all the spiritual knowledge and tools to effectively fight against the enemy.

Lest Satan should get an advantage of us: for we are not ignorant of his devices. — 2 Corinthians 2:11

Through complete deliverance and asking God to fill us with His Holy Spirit, the door is closed to the enemy and he no longer has legal right to enter unaware. We have power and authority to bind and rebuke the enemy and he will have to flee.

Submit yourselves therefore to God. Resist the devil, and he will flee from you. — James 4:7

The birth canal is a very tight space in the natural. Likewise, in the spirit, walking out this Christian journey doesn't leave room for folly, unholy living, hypocrisy, and luke warmness.

[13] Enter ye in at the strait gate: for wide is the gate, and broad is the way, that leadeth to destruction, and many there be which go in thereat:

[14] Because strait is the gate, and narrow is the way, which leadeth unto life, and few there be that find it. — Matthew 7:13-14

God gives us a choice to accept His Son as Lord and Savior of our lives. Jesus being Lord of our lives means doing His will. God wants and requires our total surrender. God sees all and knows all. Either we choose the straight and narrow way, or the wide way that leads to destruction. God will not accept us living holy on a part-time basis. We must live holy every day.

The eyes of the LORD are in every place, beholding the evil and the good. — Proverbs 15:3

[15] I know thy works, that thou art neither cold nor hot: I would thou wert cold or hot.

[16] So then because thou art lukewarm, and neither cold nor hot, I will spue thee out of my mouth. — Revelation 3:15-16

Revelation 3:15-16 (Message Bible)

"I know you inside and out and find little to my liking. You're not cold, you're not hot—far better to be either cold or hot! You're stale. You're stagnant. You make me want to vomit.

We must pray, be very diligent in our seeking God, live a holy lifestyle, and being careful to do the things that reverence and pleases Him. Everyone is ultimately responsible for their own salvation, which means no matter who around us is not living holy we must choose holiness.

Because it is written, Be ye holy; for I am holy. — 1 Peter 1:16

Wherefore, my beloved, as ye have always obeyed, not as in my presence only, but now much more in my absence, work out your own salvation with fear and trembling. — Philippians 2:12

In the natural, with the birthing process, the baby's head should lead out first. If the baby doesn't turn correctly and at the right time, the feet or buttocks may try to lead out of the birth canal, known as a breech position. Some procedures can be performed by the physician to correct this breech, but also the baby may have to be delivered via Caesarean Section. Most physicians, as well as most mothers, would rather have a vaginal delivery. If a Caesarean section has to be performed, there is more bleeding, a longer recovery time, as well as possibly lifetime scars.

In the spiritual, in a church setting, usually, the head or leader of the church is the pastor, also known as the shepherd. The other believers are members of the body of Christ and are called the sheep. The pastor, the leader, and the shepherd are appointed by God to lead and feed God's people, the sheep. Having a godly shepherd, one that is preaching and teaching the word of God, a leader that leads by example, and that bear fruit himself is a must. The sad truth is, we cannot assume that every leader is godly or living a holy life. All leaders or shepherds are not following the leading of God. All leaders or shepherds do not lead by example. Some leaders are deep into sin themselves while leading God's people. Some leaders may knowingly or unknowingly lead people unto themselves rather than to Christ. Some pastors or spiritual leaders try to control the people of God. Some do control the people of God. This is not the will of God. This is a taboo subject, but one that needs to have light shed upon. God's people perish because of a lack of knowledge. What we don't know along this Christian journey can hurt us.

⁴ Yet let no man strive, nor reprove another: for thy people are as they that strive with the priest.

⁵ Therefore shalt thou fall in the day, and the prophet also shall fall with thee in the night, and I will destroy thy mother.

⁶ My people are destroyed for lack of knowledge: because thou hast rejected knowledge, I will also reject thee, that thou shalt be no priest to me: seeing thou hast forgotten the law of thy God, I will also forget thy children.

⁷ As they were increased, so they sinned against me: therefore, will I change their glory into shame.

⁸ They eat up the sin of my people, and they set their heart on their iniquity.

⁹ And there shall be, like people, like priest: and I will punish them for their ways and reward them their doings.

¹⁰ For they shall eat, and not have enough: they shall commit whoredom, and shall not increase: because they have left off to take heed to the LORD. — Hosea 4:4-10

Hosea 4:4-10 (The Message)
⁴⁻¹⁰ "But don't look for someone to blame.
  No finger pointing!
You, priest, are the one in the dock.
  You stumble around in broad daylight,
And then the prophets take over and stumble all night.
  Your mother is as bad as you.
My people are ruined

because they don't know what's right or true.
Because you've turned your back on knowledge,
   I've turned my back on you priests.
Because you refuse to recognize the revelation of God,
   I'm no longer recognizing your children.
The more priests, the more sin.
   They traded in their glory for shame.
They pig out on my people's sins.
   They can't wait for the latest in evil.
The result: You can't tell the people from the priests,
   the priests from the people.
I'm on my way to make them both pay
   and take the consequences of the bad lives they've lived.
They'll eat and be as hungry as ever,
   have sex and get no satisfaction.
They walked out on me, their GOD,
   for a life of rutting with whores.

It is unfortunate, but if we do not have godly leadership, in the process of a believer's Christian journey, it can cause a lot of pain, spiritual bleeding and may leave lasting scars. If every leader or shepherd were godly or living holy, the Bible would not tell us to beware.

[15] Beware of false prophets, which come to you in sheep's clothing, but inwardly they are ravening wolves.

[16] Ye shall know them by their fruits. Do men gather grapes of thorns, or figs of thistles?

[17] Even so every good tree bringeth forth good fruit; but a corrupt tree bringeth forth evil fruit.

[18] A good tree cannot bring forth evil fruit, neither can a corrupt tree bring forth good fruit. — Matthew 7:15-18

It is each believer's responsibility to make sure that their leader who is watching over their soul is a fully submitted vessel of God. Every Christian needs sound, balanced, Biblical teaching, and guidance. I say this because if not careful, in our eagerness to please God, the enemy can slip in, unaware in seemingly righteous ways. The Bible tells us to obey and submit to spiritual authority.

Obey them that have the rule over you and submit yourselves: for they watch for your souls, as they that must give account, that they may do it with joy, and not with grief: for that is unprofitable for you.— Hebrews 13:17

We are to submit and obey, but not to allow the pastor/spiritual leader to become an idol. Sometimes, through our zeal and yearning for God, we may unknowingly submit to a leader, and almost idolize them. They are not our God. Sometimes in our submitting, we allow ourselves to be controlled unaware. Some pastors/spiritual leaders are full of pride and very controlling. We should not allow ourselves to be controlled by a spiritual leader/pastor, or anyone else for that matter. No one has the right to control another person. God doesn't force us to serve Him. He gives us a choice whether to serve Him or serve the devil. Likewise, pastors/spiritual leaders have no right to control, manipulate, nor dominate God's people. The sheep are God's sheep, not the pastor's sheep. When a pastor/spiritual leader try to control the flock/sheep, whether knowingly or unknowingly, that is Charismatic witchcraft. We know witchcraft has to do with mind control and is of the enemy.

One definition of charismatic witchcraft is when a leader or someone within the church exercises control over the flock/sheep. Most commonly, the pastor/spiritual leader is the one that exerts control or manipulation over the congregation.

I speak, not from bitterness, but from experience because I have been on the receiving end of charismatic witchcraft, which at the time, I did not know existed. I did not know witchcraft existed in the church, but it does. We, as God's people, look to the pastor/spiritual leader to help us walk out or do the will of God. We look to the pastor/leader to shepherd us to grow us in the things of God. Most often, when God's people are being dominated or controlled, it's because they trusted that leader. The trust that is put in the pastor/spiritual leaders can be used by them in the wrong way. That trust can be taken advantage of and manipulated into serving man's will and not God's will. This is not to say all leaders/pastors will take advantage of the sheep, but some will. When we sit under and allow ourselves as Christians to be dominated, manipulated or controlled by any spiritual leader/person, we are unknowingly and sometimes, knowingly coming into agreement with that control, which is a sin. When a Christian submits themselves to such control or domination from the pastor/leader, soul ties are formed with the pastor/spiritual leader.

In the secular world, patients trust their doctors. Therefore, the patients are vulnerable to their doctors. In the church world, the people of God can be vulnerable to pastors/spiritual leaders when their trust is manipulated to further the leader's/pastor's own agenda. A controlling pastor/leader can easily exploit this vulnerability and trust. Exploitation can lead the people of God into a place of confusion, hurt, and shame. Some Christians may even walk away from God because of "church hurt." Some may or may not find their way back to God.

If the pastor/spiritual leader is controlling, it is not the will of God to remain under that type of witchcraft. I have been associated with controlling pastors/spiritual leaders, through my association, I did not walk away from God, but the experience was very difficult to escape from and took a few years to break free. I did not know I was dealing with an ungodly soul tie that had formed with my then pastor/spiritual leader. I had no training in spiritual warfare. I had been dominated and controlled by my ex-husband. I lived mostly in constant fear of him and his abuse. Aside from the soul tie with him, I allowed myself to be dominated and controlled by him for almost seven years, which had formed an ungodly soul tie. After I left him, I had no idea that I needed deliverance from fear and other demonic spirits that the domination had caused in my life. Since I had not repented, renounced, fallen out of agreement, and broken those ungodly soul ties with my ex-husband, those doors were still open. The open doors may have allowed the enemy an entry point to re-enter years later though taking another form, charismatic witchcraft.

When trying desperately to obey God and those that rule over you, there is a fine line. That fine line reads we should always obey God, first and foremost. If the one that has rule over you is not obeying God, then we are not to obey them. God is the ultimate ruler and has the ultimate rule.

Then Peter and the other apostles answered and said, We ought to obey God rather than men. — Acts 5:29

I served a pastor/leader in this particular ministry faithfully. Over the years, I saw things that were not right, but I shrugged them off. In this ministry, the power of God would move in the services. I could not understand how God would come and visit us in these services if things were being done out of His will. Control and domination are not right. It's a sin. But God is a merciful God. The years went by and nothing changed when it came to the control issue. But something changed in me. I became more uncomfortable seeing and knowing that God was not pleased with this situation and felt that something was going to have to change. Also, I noticed that I was not being fulfilled. Neither was I growing in the ministry any longer. The

Holy Ghost would come in our services, but I had a knowing that He wanted to come in a greater way. I had become so hungry and thirsty for more of God that I yearned to see His power in a higher dimension. I longed to see miracles, signs, and wonders.

[17] And these signs shall follow them that believe; In my name shall they cast out devils; they shall speak with new tongues;

[18] They shall take up serpents; and if they drink any deadly thing, it shall not hurt them; they shall lay hands on the sick, and they shall recover. — Mark 16:17-18

We were believers, so why didn't we seeing these things in our services? God is the same God. What He did back then, He will do today if we are truly living for Him. I was hungry for a mighty move of God where miracles, signs, and wonders are following and manifested. Not just a visit every now and then. I wanted to see souls saved, completely delivered, and set free. I hungered for the fullness of God because I was no longer satisfied with just a touch from Him. I thirsted to know God deeper.

Blessed are they which do hunger and thirst after righteousness: for they shall be filled. — Matthew 5:6

I hungered, thirsted, prayed and interceded for God to come in and take full control. I knew we needed revival. Through prayer, I felt that something was hindering God's Spirit in the church and not allowing Him to have His way.

[19] Quench not the Spirit.
[20] Despise not prophesyings.
[21] Prove all things; hold fast that which is good.
[22] Abstain from all appearance of evil. — 1 Thessalonians 5:19-22

1 Thessalonians 5:19-22 (The Message)

[19-22] Don't suppress the Spirit, and don't stifle those who have a word from the Master. On the other hand, don't be gullible. Check out everything and keep only what's good. Throw out anything tainted with evil.

These Scriptures let me know the spirit of God was being quenched. Something was hindering His move and not allowing Him to have His way. He plainly tells us to abstain from all appearance of evil. In simpler terms, throw out anything that is tainted with evil. The word was also telling us not to be gullible. If I remained silent any longer concerning sin being committed and allow it, I was being gullible and not throwing out what was tainted. I knew it was not completely in my hands to correct things at the church, but it was in my hands whether to remain under this type of control. I knew the spirit was being quenched. I knew that controlling the congregation was wrong, so now what do I do. After much prayer, I felt led to ask for a meeting with the pastor/leader of the church. I don't know what I expected, but I needed to voice what I felt the Lord was saying about why spiritual growth and the manifestation of God was being hindered. I knew that if we set things right at the church with God, He would forgive and heal what needed healing. The Lord gave me 2 Chronicles 7:14 in 7 a.m. prayer one Saturday morning while praying for the church service the next day. Repentance was a must if we were to be healed and see revival and it must begin with the leader/pastor.

[12] And the LORD appeared to Solomon by night, and said unto him, I have heard thy prayer, and have chosen this place to myself for a house of sacrifice.

[13] If I shut up heaven that there be no rain, or if I command the locusts to devour the land, or if I send pestilence among my people;

[14] If my people, which are called by my name, shall humble themselves, and pray, and seek my face, and turn from their wicked ways;

then will I hear from heaven, and will forgive their sin, and will heal their land. — 2 Chronicles 7:12-14

2 Chronicles 7:12-14 (The Message)

[12-14] GOD appeared to Solomon that very night and said, "I accept your prayer; yes, I have chosen this place as a temple for sacrifice, a house of worship. If I ever shut off the supply of rain from the skies or order the locusts to eat the crops or send a plague on my people, and my people, my God-defined people, respond by humbling themselves, praying, seeking my presence, and turning their backs on their wicked lives, I'll be there ready for you: I'll listen from heaven, forgive their sins, and restore their land to health.

We needed our land restored to health. Therefore we would have to turn from our wicked ways, pray, and see God. It's hard to think that we as God's people have some wicked way, but we do, and this includes the preachers of the gospel as well as all others.

The meeting I requested with the pastor/leader was granted. I met with him and told him what I felt God wanted me to tell him. He listened, but evidently, he didn't receive the severity of the message I carried. The message was that for God to do what He wants to do in our midst, repentance will be the only thing that God will accept. In the days, months and about three years to come, nothing changed at the church as far as repentance. Actually, things got worse. As a matter of fact, for me, things became unbearable and I knew what I had to do to do God's will and get some peace of mind. I made up my mind that I was not going to accept being dominated, manipulated, and controlled any longer. I was wrong to allow it for as long as I had. Every decision I made was from much prayer. Seemingly the only recourse out of the turmoil and to obey God was to disassociate from the church and the leader/pastor.

I requested a second meeting with the pastor/leader and it was granted. In this meeting, I had to respectfully say things that should have been said so many years before. I told this pastor/leader that I was not getting what I needed in the services, was not growing, and desired to see God do mighty things in my life as well as others. I told him that I felt that the Lord was saying the strongholds that had been built up over the years because of his sins and the fact that he refused to repent. I let him know that I could not remain in the ministry any long unless things changed, namely repentance and allowing God to do great and mighty things in the ministry. I let him know that I was not going to allow myself to be dominated any longer. I thought there would be repentance, but again, it did not happen. I allowed space for repentance, but he did not feel he needed to repent. Some leaders/pastors are prideful and have a problem with repenting. Pastors/spiritual leaders should be the first to repent. 2 Chronicles 7:14 refers to the people called by the name of the Lord. The pastor/leaders are called by the name of the Lord. Therefore, they are not exempt from humbling themselves.

Let the priests, the ministers of the LORD, weep between the porch and the altar, and let them say, Spare thy people, O LORD, and give not thine heritage to reproach, that the heathen should rule over them: wherefore should they say among the people, Where is their God? — Joel 2:17

Since there was no repentance, it was now time to remove myself from under that leadership, so I did. It was no other alternative at this point. God let me know that strongholds had been erected over the years through the unrepentant sins that had been committed and that were yet being committed. These strongholds were blocking a free-flowing move of God. Stronghold are wrong thoughts and perceptions, contradicting the true knowledge of God and His nature. These strongholds needed to be pulled down in the spirit realm.

³ For though we walk in the flesh, we do not war after the flesh:

⁴ (For the weapons of our warfare are not carnal, but mighty through God to the pulling down of strong holds;)

⁵ Casting down imaginations, and every high thing that exalteth itself against the knowledge of God, and bringing into captivity every thought to the obedience of Christ;

⁶ And having in a readiness to revenge all disobedience, when your obedience is fulfilled. — 2 Corinthians 10:3-6

2 Corinthians 10:3-6 (The Message)

³⁻⁶ The world is unprincipled. It's dog-eat-dog out there! The world doesn't fight fair. But we don't live or fight our battles that way—never have and never will. The tools of our trade aren't for marketing or manipulation, but they are for demolishing that entire massively corrupt culture. We use our powerful God-tools for smashing warped philosophies, tearing down barriers erected against the truth of God, fitting every loose thought and emotion and impulse into the structure of life shaped by Christ. Our tools are ready at hand for clearing the ground of every obstruction and building lives of obedience into maturity.

CHAPTER 6

THE BREACH

The decision to leave the ministry and that leadership was not easy. I had been there for more than twenty years. I had allowed myself, and in a sense, unwillingly came into agreement with things that were not pleasing to God by remaining there such a long time. I would need a renewing of the mind because I had conformed to that culture, the way things were done, and listened to things that were said. I had been taught that being a part of this particular ministry could bless or curse. For so long, I was afraid to voice my opinion to this spiritual leader, so I remained quiet. I was scared to go against what this leader said. For one reason, I thought that whatever the spiritual leader said, it was coming from God. Therefore, I felt if I disagreed in any way with this leader that I was disagreeing with God. I was afraid of getting rebuked if I disagreed with this leader. The culture or mentality of this spiritual leader/congregation relationship was that if one disagreed with whatever the leader said or did, they were not with the program.

Through the years, I felt I was rebelling against God if I did not obey the leader, even though some of the things he did were wrong. I knew somewhere in my spirit that this type of atmosphere was not right. I thought that if I left this particular congregation, I would be walking away from God, would lose my salvation, and would not be blessed if I left this ministry. I learned later that if I did not leave this ministry, I would not be blessed. Control and manipulation were strongly used in the area of offerings and finances while being a part of this congregation. I had been sowing lots of seeds over the years, but I didn't seem to be reaping from it. The Bible tells us that God's loves a cheerful giver. Giving should never be coerced or manipulated. We should not give because we are embarrassed, forced, or manipulated into giving. That is not biblical; therefore, it is not the will of God.

In the beginning, I willingly gave whatever was expected because I felt that's what God required. I was told that is what God said and wanted. But as time went on, I sometimes gave because I was afraid not to give. I grew tired of sowing, but I kept giving even though it seemed that I was not being blessed by giving. In a sense, I felt sowing sacrificial seeds had become a learned behavior. It was expected, so I continued to make sacrificial offerings. Even when it seemed I was not reaping, I continued to sow thousands of dollars. I wanted to stop, but I was afraid not to give, again, that's not the will of God. While I was a part of this congregation, I was manipulated into more than one money-making schemes called investments, in which I lost money. By this time, I had gained enough strength to let it be known that I did not want to spend my money on those types of investments. I was not taken seriously, and I was yet expected to invest in gimmicks the leader/pastor presented to the congregation. Even after losing money, we as members of the congregation were still expected to do whatever was asked of them by the leader, without question. There were different tactics or projects used to get the people of God to give.

But through maturity and drawing close to God, I eventually learned that if the pastor/preacher/spiritual leader is trying to manipulate the people to give against the believer's will, that is contrary to God's word. We, as the people of God, do not have to obey that leader in that instance. Even when it comes to finances/offerings, the Bible lets us know that we decide in our own heart what to give. It is not the will of God for the pastor/spiritual leader to coerce or manipulate any person in the congregation to give finances or do anything against that person's will. When manipulation is used, we are not required by God to obey that leader, and God will bear us up.

Every man according as he purposeth in his heart, so let him give; not grudgingly, or of necessity: for God loveth a cheerful giver. — 2 Corinthians 9:7

2 Corinthians 9:7 (The Message)
I want each of you to take plenty of time to think it over and make up your own mind what you will give. That will protect you against sob stories and arm-twisting. God loves it when the giver delights in the giving.

By the leading of the Holy Ghost, I left a job that I had been on for ten years. I thought the main reason I left that job was that I was tired of giving money. I felt that if I wasn't working at this particular place, I would not have the amount of money that was required of me to give. Because still, at this time, I was afraid not to give what was expected. I began to pray like never before. I began to read and study my Bible. I was so hungry for God and in need of direction. I read the entire Bible in less than a year. If we seek God, He will make His will known to us. He will give us clarity in our thinking. I sought God early most mornings at 5 a.m. prayer. I sought Him and He met me and ministered to me. I had no one to go to for spiritual counseling. But I found out I had the best counselor, the Holy Ghost. Since I could not understand why I wasn't being blessed after everything I had sowed into this ministry, I found the answer. Through my studying the Word of God, I discovered that God's people should not give tithes on unholy altars. I had given tithes in this ministry for twenty years. I began to wonder if I was giving my tithes on unholy altars because of the things that God was not pleased with that was going on in this ministry. The Bible lets us know that we must give our tithes on holy altars if we want God to bless.

Even when I felt God was leading me to move from that ministry, I doubted that I was hearing God correctly. I was so confused from being controlled. It was hard to believe God was talking to me, and not through the pastor/spiritual leader. But God let me know that, yes, He was talking to me. That's what eventually led me to leave this ministry. I feel God was showing me that the greed, pride, arrogance, lying, and manipulation was going to continue, and I would be under those strongholds and would not be blessed if I did not leave this ministry.

I knew my heart was right. I had no guile nor desire to be vengeful. So, I left with a love for the leader. I had spoken with the leader twice as led by God, and I left the ministry in a godly fashion. I have much love for that leader even to this day. He is a good person, and whether knowingly or unknowingly on his part, wrongs were committed and needed to be made right. The pastor/leader did not repent because he did not feel he had anything to repent of; nevertheless, I forgave/forgive him. I felt used and hurt, but I know God will judge.

When David went out to meet them, this is what he said: "If you have come in peace and to help me, you are most welcome to join this company; but if you have come to betray me to my enemies, innocent as I am, the God of our ancestors will see through you and bring judgment on you."— 1 Chronicles 12:17

God requires us to forgive, even if the person that wronged us does not ask for forgiveness. Forgiveness is for the person being sinned against, not for the person that commits the sin.

For if you forgive others their trespasses, your heavenly Father will also forgive you, but if you do not forgive others their trespasses, neither will your Father forgive your trespasses. — Matthew 6:14-15

Therefore, I forgave him and began to pray God's mercy on him because we all must reap what we sow. God was calling me to another place in Him and I could not answer that call, had I remained in that ministry. There were too many strongholds there and I would not be blessed there as it were. I must thank God for the time I spent in that ministry. Whatever transpired during my time there, God will use it for my good. If I could turn back time, I would not repeat those same mistakes.

In everything give thanks: for this is the will of God in Christ Jesus concerning you. — 1 Thessalonians 5:18

And we know that all things work together for good to those who love God, to those who are the called according to His purpose. — Romans 8:28

Through it all, what I did receive while in that ministry was an impartation for prayer, and for that, I'm forever grateful. I learned how to work the altar and pray the souls through that were seeking God. I'm thankful for the 9 a.m. prayers with the missionaries and prayer warriors. I'm grateful for the 12 a.m. shut-ins with the prayer warriors. The Lord also blessed me with a lifetime friend while I was at this ministry and we remain friends to this day.

I obeyed God when I left the ministry. That was the will of God for me. As I begin a more in-depth study of spiritual warfare, I realized I needed to break some word curses concerning anyone that left that ministry. That revelation would come later. Again, I did not know and would find out years later that I needed to repent for allowing myself to be dominated, manipulated, and controlled once again. I would need to renounce and fall out of alignment with any person that I gave that type of control in my life. I had to break the ungodly soul ties that had been formed through the connection. If I had received the discerning of spirits when I received the Holy Ghost, I could have possibly saved myself a lot of anguish and manipulation. In retrospect, God had warned me several times over the years of things that He was not pleased with in that particular ministry, but I did not heed His warnings. For that, I had to repent. I pray that by me sharing what I endured by allowing myself to be controlled by a pastor/spiritual leader, it will bring awareness and hopefully save others from succumbing to charismatic witchcraft. God did not deliver and bring me out for me to keep silent.

Immediately after salvation, believers should ask God to be filled with the Holy Spirit. After being filled with the Holy Spirit, they should desire and pray for all the gifts of the Spirit to operate in their lives. When I gave my life to Jesus, I prayed to receive the baptism of the Holy Spirit. However, after I received the baptism of the Holy Spirit, I did not know that I needed all the gifts that come with being filled with Him. I spoke in tongues, but that was the only gift that I had operating in my life. The other gifts were not emphasized or taught at length. Therefore after receiving the gift of tongues, I was satisfied with that one gift.

I read my Bible, but I did not understand a lot of the things I read. I had mostly relied on what my leader at the time said God was saying. I did not know at that time that God speaks to us individually as well, independent from our pastors/leaders. Sometimes, the fact that God speaks to everyone may not be respected and taught by our leaders, especially controlling leaders. Sometimes we are just expected to do what we are told to do. Not enough or hardly any emphasis is put on hearing God for ourselves in every situation and seeking Him for the discerning of spirits.

⁷ But the manifestation of the Spirit is given to every man to profit withal.

⁸ For to one is given by the Spirit the word of wisdom; to another the word of knowledge by the same Spirit;

⁹ To another faith by the same Spirit; to another the gifts of healing by the same Spirit;

¹⁰ To another the working of miracles; to another prophecy; to another discerning of spirits; to another divers kinds of tongues; to another the interpretation of tongues:

¹¹ But all these worketh that one and the selfsame Spirit, dividing to every man severally as he will. — 1 Corinthians 12:7-11

All these spiritual gifts are very important to our walk with God, but I would strongly suggest praying for the discerning of spirits immediately because it will help us. Had I the gift of discerning of spirits operating in my life, I could have avoided a lot of heartache and pains in my walk with God earlier on in my salvation. My journey through the birthing process was breached in hindsight. I did not have all the knowledge that I feel I needed to maintain my deliverance and I came into agreement with being controlled for several years. I thought that after I gave my life to God, things that I had struggled with would somehow work themselves out. I was wrong because Satan is cunning and very strategic. For instance, I had gotten forgiveness for lust, but I had never renounced it. I never fell out of agreement with the lust spirit, leading me to fornication a few years after my confessing Christ. I never fell out of agreement and broke the soul ties to my ex-husband from the abuse. There was no teaching on the process of deliverance from certain sins from the past.

Sometimes the people of God feel comfortable preaching, teaching, and praying against drugs, but the lust spirit sometimes gets little or no attention. Likewise, charismatic witchcraft gets little or no attention at all. I found out years later in my salvation that all the men with whom I had sexual relations, soul ties were developed and needed to be broken. All ungodly soul ties needed to be broken. I found through an intensive study on spiritual warfare that the door needed to be closed so the enemy would not have the legal right to enter back in. I discovered through the leading of the Holy Spirit about spiritual warfare. The people of God need to be taught in detail about spiritual warfare and the many wiles of the enemy. Christians need to be taught about the power and authority we have through Christ Jesus and how to fight the enemy. We cannot fight in our own strength. We need the power of God operating in our lives. And we need to use the authority given to us by God.

For we wrestle not against flesh and blood, but against principalities, against powers, against the rulers of the darkness of this world, against spiritual wickedness in high places. — Ephesians 6:12

Behold, I give unto you power to tread on serpents and scorpions, and over all the power of the enemy: and nothing shall by any means hurt you. — Luke 10:19

I would have avoided some of the deliverance pains and roadblocks if I knew then what I know now, if I had listened to God, and if I had not doubted that God was speaking and leading me. I encountered this because of willful sin and unwilful sins, and because of ignorance. I could have saved myself from so much warfare had I known that it's more to be done even after we repent. Yes, if we repent, God is faithful to forgive us. But what doors were opened by our sinful actions? Whether we got caught up in sin, knowingly or unknowingly, the consequence is the same. There may have been doors opened that gave the enemy the legal right to attack us. Through our sins, demonic doors were opened. Therefore, we may need to do warfare to close those doors. We need to confess, renounce, and fall out of alignment with the sin. Next, ask God for forgiveness for the sin, and accept it. We must be diligent to not allow condemnation, guilt, and shame to set up in our spirits. The Word tells us in Romans 8:1-2, There is therefore now no condemnation to them which are in Christ Jesus, who walk not after the flesh, but after the Spirit. For the law of the Spirit of life in Christ Jesus hath made me free from the law of sin and death.

I felt condemnation for the sins I committed and for allowing myself to be manipulated, which is a sin. I struggled with how I could have allowed those things to happen since I had given my life to Christ. But through ignorance and not being completely delivered and healed from my past, I entered a backslidden state, yet still professing salvation. Teaching and training were not available to me. But I just kept humbling myself and repenting and that's how I had no other desire but to stay in the race. This Christian journey is a process. We cannot run the race in one day, but must endure until the end. We must be repentant, patient, and rely on the Holy Spirit every day to lead and guide us.

I returned, and saw under the sun, that the race is not to the swift, nor the battle to the strong, neither yet bread to the wise, nor yet riches to men of understanding, nor yet favour to men of skill; but time and chance happeneth to them all. — Ecclesiastes 9:11

Provisions have already been made before the foundations of the world. God knew we were going to fall into sin sometimes, but He made it, so we don't have to stay in a fallen state, we can and must repent and do our first work over. Repent means to turn from the situation that caused the fall. If we are sincere, we should pray and ask

God for strength and help in our daily journey towards perfection. If we want to live holy, God is right there to help us. The Holy Ghost is our keeper, and He will keep us if we furnish the will to be kept from sin. It is such a misconception of a lot of Christian's part in thinking that once saved, always saved. Some think we can give our lives to the Lord, and then for whatever reason, we backslide, return to sin, continue to live sinful lives, and refuse to repent. The misconception is to think we can still go to heaven. That's not a part of the plan of salvation. God did not send His Son from glory to give His life to save us, and then we do not accept Him with our whole heart. We must remain faithful to God's statues. It is a process, one day at a time. If we do not repent of our sins, God will surely judge us.

"Remember therefore from whence thou art fallen, and repent, and do the first works; or else I will come unto thee quickly, and will remove thy candlestick out of his place, except thou repent." — Revelation 2:5

There was no manual when I accepted salvation on what to look for and be aware of. There was no one telling me who to look out for. There was no teaching of what was of God and what was not of God. It was implied, yet unspoken that just giving one's life to the Lord and getting filled with the Holy Ghost should keep us from sin. Some of us came up out of a horrible pit. Some of us have been in that pit for more than 30 years. The power of God is powerful, and we will receive it after that the Holy Ghost comes upon us. There could be some things in the spirit realm that may hinder a person's full deliverance, such as strongholds that are standing in their way.

Deliverance workers that are fully submitted to God are needed to walk new Christians through deliverance by teaching and training them. They should have a heart for God and with a heart after God, which cannot be stressed enough. The new Christian doesn't have the keen discernment immediately after accepting Christ as Lord and Savior. They are feeling their way. Sometimes we are too hard and demanding with them. They make mistakes as we all do. We can't assume that they are where we are and as strong as we are. It took a lot for some of us to get where we are in God. We fell into some things that were displeasing to God, but after we repented, God forgave and restored us. The mature people in the Lord should advise the immature ones on what and who to be aware of on this journey.

[1] We then that are strong ought to bear the infirmities of the weak, and not to please ourselves.
[2] Let every one of us please his neighbour for his good to edification. —Romans 15:1-2

Romans 15 (The Message)
[1-2] Those of us who are strong and able in the faith need to step in and lend a hand to those who falter, and not just do what is most convenient for us. Strength is for service, not status. Each one of us needs to look after the good of the people around us, asking ourselves, "How can I help?"

There is no time to cover for sin, to compromise with the enemy, and to be concerned about offending other people by being truthful and doing the will of the Lord. It offends God when we sin against Him and neglect to do His will. So, it's better to offend man than offend God. Souls are at stake. We do not want their blood on our hands. Therefore, we are commissioned by God to warn people of their sin and short comings. Also, we should then show them the way back to salvation. If we know someone is being taken advantage of or is at risk of being taken advantage of, it is our duty to warn them as well. God expects us to expose sin and to be a light in darkness.

¹⁷ Son of man, I have made thee a watchman unto the house of Israel: therefore, hear the word at my mouth, and give them warning from me.

¹⁸ When I say unto the wicked, Thou shalt surely die; and thou givest him not warning, nor speakest to warn the wicked from his wicked way, to save his life; the same wicked man shall die in his iniquity; but his blood will I require at thine hand.

¹⁹ Yet if thou warn the wicked, and he turn not from his wickedness, nor from his wicked way, he shall die in his iniquity; but thou hast delivered thy soul. — Ezekiel 3:17-19

The Message (Ezekiel 3:17-19)

¹⁷⁻¹⁹ "Son of man, I've made you a watchman for the family of Israel. Whenever you hear me say something, warn them for me. If I say to the wicked, 'You are going to die,' and you don't sound the alarm warning them that it's a matter of life or death, they will die and it will be your fault. I'll hold you responsible. But if you warn the wicked and they keep right on sinning anyway, they'll most certainly die for their sin, but you won't die. You'll have saved your life.

I paid the price for the knowledge that I gained. I was hurt by learning these many lessons. I made a lot of mistakes growing into maturity and in the knowledge of the things of God. It took some of the mistakes to help pray and seek God for the discerning of spirits. Some of the struggles I went through, I didn't come out bitter, I came out with a determination that nothing and no one is worth my relationship with God. I came out with a made-up mind that I was going to serve God whole heartedly. I was through being lukewarm. I didn't want God to spew me out of His mouth for being neither hot nor cold.

When I found myself without a church home, without a pastor/ spiritual to watch over my soul, I had nobody but God. I continued in prayer for direction. I knew God was calling me to a place in Him that I had never been, but how do I get there with no spiritual guidance? I was hungry and thirsty for more of God. And I knew God was not going to not fill that hunger and quench that thirst I had for Him. I wanted to move in the things of God. I wanted to help if I could in other's deliverance. I desired to help pray others into their breakthroughs. But where do I go as far as a deliverance ministry? I had declared that I would not be controlled again by any pastor/leader. I would have to use discernment this time and follow God's direction. In the meantime, I visited a couple of churches. I did not feel led to go from church to church, being susceptible to picking up strange spirits. I needed somewhere where the glory of God is really welcome. I needed to be a part of a church where holiness was a lifestyle. The leader would need to be humble before God, and shepherd His people with love. The pastor/leader would need to have integrity. I refused to associate with a pastor/spiritual leader that had a form of godliness but denying the power thereof. The hour is late, and the time is short. Jesus is soon to come.

[1] This know also, that in the last days perilous times shall come.

[2] For men shall be lovers of their own selves, covetous, boasters, proud, blasphemers, disobedient to parents, unthankful, unholy,

[3] Without natural affection, trucebreakers, false accusers, incontinent, fierce, despisers of those that are good,

[4] Traitors, heady, highminded, lovers of pleasures more than lovers of God;

[5] Having a form of godliness, but denying the power thereof: from such turn away.

[6] For of this sort are they which creep into houses, and lead captive silly women laden with sins, led away with divers lusts,

[7] Ever learning, and never able to come to the knowledge of the truth.

[8] Now as Jannes and Jambres withstood Moses, so do these also resist the truth: men of corrupt minds, reprobate concerning the faith.

⁹ But they shall proceed no further: for their folly shall be manifest unto all men, as their's also was. — 2 Timothy 3:1-9

The Message (2 Timothy 3:1-9)
¹⁻⁵ Don't be naive. There are difficult times ahead. As the end approaches, people are going to be self-absorbed, money-hungry, self-promoting, stuck-up, profane, contemptuous of parents, crude, coarse, dog-eat-dog, unbending, slanderers, impulsively wild, savage, cynical, treacherous, ruthless, bloated windbags, addicted to lust, and allergic to God. They'll make a show of religion, but behind the scenes they're animals. Stay clear of these people.

⁶⁻⁹ These are the kind of people who smooth-talk themselves into the homes of unstable and needy women and take advantage of them; women who, depressed by their sinfulness, take up with every new religious fad that calls itself "truth." They get exploited every time and never really learn. These men are like those old Egyptian frauds Jannes and Jambres, who challenged Moses. They were rejects from the faith, twisted in their thinking, defying truth itself. But nothing will come of these latest impostors. Everyone will see through them, just as people saw through that Egyptian hoax.

I have heard that there are no perfect churches/pastors. I'm not looking for a perfect church. I'm looking for a leader/ministry that is after the heart of God and has a heart for His people. I'm looking for a church/pastor/leader that is a threat to Satan's kingdom. I need a spiritual leader that is doing the will of God and that will not compromise. I'm looking for someone that will not use God's people to further their agenda but to further the kingdom of God. I need a leader that will help propel me into the things that God has for the congregation and me. I need a leader that, if I'm wrong, I expect rebuke that's done in love. I don't have the grace to align myself with a pastor/spiritual leader that is hungry for fame, a platform, money, and the things of the world. My heart is pure before God, and I expect no less from whoever is to watch over my soul. I know and understand that every person in the congregation is not a believer, nor is everyone walking upright before God. But God did not call the congregation to lead and feed His sheep. He called pastors. My focus is on the pastor/leader because he is the leader. The pastor is the one assigned to watch after my soul and give an account, not the congregation. Pastors/spiritual leaders are held to a higher standard because of their position. He should be above reproach.

[1] This is a true saying, if a man desire the office of a bishop, he desireth a good work.

[2] A bishop then must be blameless, the husband of one wife, vigilant, sober, of good behaviour, given to hospitality, apt to teach;

[3] Not given to wine, no striker, not greedy of filthy lucre; but patient, not a brawler, not covetous;

[4] One that ruleth well his own house, having his children in subjection with all gravity;

[5] (For if a man know not how to rule his own house, how shall he take care of the church of God?)

[6] Not a novice, lest being lifted up with pride he fall into the condemnation of the devil.

[7] Moreover he must have a good report of them which are without; lest he fall into reproach and the snare of the devil. — 1 Timothy 3:1-7

1 Timothy 3:1-7 (The Message)

[1-7] If anyone wants to provide leadership in the church, good! But there are preconditions: A leader must be well-thought-of, committed to his wife, cool and collected, accessible, and hospitable.

He must know what he's talking about, not be over fond of wine, not pushy but gentle, not thin-skinned, not money hungry. He must handle his own affairs well, attentive to his own children and having their respect.

For if someone is unable to handle his own affairs, how can he take care of God's church? He must not be a new believer, lest the position go to his head and the Devil trip him up. Outsiders must think well of him, or else the Devil will figure out a way to lure him into his trap.

The burning desire that I have for God, I will not settle for religion, or just going to church and not growing in Him. I discerned some things that I wasn't willing to align myself with at the churches that I visited. I continued in prayer for God to lead me to the right place. In the meantime, I begin to watch church services on LIVE stream by anointed men of God. I watched YouTube sermons from powerful men and women of God. I listen to prayers from mighty prayer warriors and intercessors on YouTube, which kept my relationship with God strong. I know we are not to forsake assembling ourselves, so every so often, I went to a church service, even though when I left sometimes, I was not fulfilled. I needed the glory of God to rest in worship service, but sometimes, God was not allowed to have His way. There were people of God that needed to be delivered, but the church services didn't always include deliverance.

Not forsaking the assembling of ourselves together, as the manner of some is; but exhorting one another: and so much the more, as ye see the day approaching. —Hebrews 10:25

I know God doesn't like religion because He wants us to have a personal relationship with Him. I had to get to know Him in a deeper way. Like King David, I longed for God's presence and a more intimate relationship with Him. What I really needed is revival because we all need it. I wanted to see souls saved, bodies healed, delivered, and set free, but most of all, God's name to be glorified in all the earth. Preaching a nice sermon is good, but it cannot replace the glory of God. We not only need the preached Word, but we also need it with demonstration.

¹ As the hart panteth after the water brooks, so panteth my soul after thee, O God.

² My soul thirsteth for God, for the living God: when shall I come and appear before God? —Psalms 42:1-2

I wondered when God would lead me to where this hunger for thirst will be satisfied. When would He lead me to a church where He is moving mightily? I was in a hurry to find a church home, a pastor/leader, but I did not want to run ahead of God's leading. I wanted to obey God and assemble myself with other saints, but where do I go? I feel that aligning with just any church just to say I do go to church is not the will of God for me. God will never contradict His word concerning anything. He says that we should assemble together and that's His word. He did not say how often to assemble ourselves, whether once a week, once a month, twice a week, how often?

Concerning this issue for me, (this is only for me, each individual will need to seek God concerning His will for their selves) I feel God showed me a scenario in the natural and a scenario pertaining to the spiritual. In the natural, if I am in the military, and I deploy to the desert of Afghanistan, possibly combat for six months to a year, most likely, I would not be attending church services. What do I do in that situation as far as my relationship with God? I could not just lay my salvation aside until I get back to the states. If in that situation, God would not reject me or leave me alone, but He would be with me even more. It would be just God and me. I would still fast, pray, and read my Bible as often as I could until I returned. The scenario in the spiritual is, whether I'm in church service every Sunday or once a month, I am required to keep my relationship with God strong, fasting, praying, studying my Bible and doing whatever I can to stay close to Him. Because I am a soldier, I am in spiritual combat and enlisted in the army of the Lord. He has called me to fight through intercession because intercessors are front line soldiers. I am an end time warrior. The revelation that came out of that scenario is that God has me in a place of hiding and a place of pruning right now. The reason I have not connected with a church/spiritual leader yet is that I cannot be aligned with just any pastor/spiritual leader or church. God has chosen me for a special work in these last days. God is getting His army ready. He wants humble, yet bold soldiers. God needs someone after His heart and that will not compromise. He needs someone that is pure and holy. Also, someone that loves Him and His people. God desires someone that is hungry for more than just a program, but hungry for a revolutionary move of His Spirit and glory, continually.

Therefore, God gave me peace, understanding, and patience concerning me not having a spiritual leader/pastor/church. He let me know the Holy Ghost is covering, leading, guiding, and raising me up. When the time is right, God will reveal where He wants me to serve and under what leadership. Often, when a spiritual leader helps groom a spiritual daughter/son, that leader wants the glory. They want the credit for being their leader and training them. I say this with all humility, but the glory that is going to be revealed in my life and the lives of others for being obedient to God. Only the Holy Ghost will get the glory. I have known for years that I was called to be a prayer warrior. I love prayer and loved to pray. It has not always been that way, but through my seeking to please God, He says we should always pray.

And he spake a parable unto them to this end, that men ought always to pray, and not to faint; — Luke 18:1

Pray without ceasing. — 1 Thess. 5:17

Praying always with all prayer and supplication in the Spirit, and watching thereunto with all perseverance and supplication for all saints; — Ephesians 6:18

There is power in agreement, but I did not know anyone in my area that yearned for pray as I did or that would agree with me in prayer. I don't mean praying a few minutes or going through the motions of prayer. I mean laboring in prayer. Prayer is work and sacrifice. Travailing prayer it is not cute. We need a burden for prayer and be willing to humble ourselves. We need a repentant heart and a contrite spirit because we want our prayers to be effective.

Confess your faults one to another, and pray one for another, that ye may be healed. The effectual fervent prayer of a righteous man availeth much. — James 5:16

Again I say unto you, That if two of you shall agree on earth as touching anything that they shall ask, it shall be done for them of my Father which is in heaven — Matthew 18:19

The only person that I know that loves prayer and was also a called and chosen prayer warrior was my daughter Merlendi, that lived four hours away. She is saved, for real, sanctified, Holy Ghost filled and fire baptized. She is a young lady with a pure heart and loves God with all her might. God had led her away from the ministry she had been in since college, and she had no church home at the time either. God was calling us both to a place in Him that not many people understood. But we obey God, not man. God will get the glory for our lives what He is doing. We began to pray together almost every day over the phone. As we continued in prayer, God began to put a burden in our hearts for certain people. We would pray for those people until God gave us a release.

After a while, we both felt that God was calling us even deeper in prayer. He was leading us into intercession. There is so much going on in the world that it's crazy such as school massacres, church massacres, road rage, domestic violence, suicides, murder-suicides, bullying, hot car deaths, and the list goes on. If it were not for God, we would not make it. We would lose our minds and live in utter fear. But God did not give us the spirit of fear.

For God hath not given us the spirit of fear; but of power, and of love, and of a sound mind. — 2 Timothy 1:7

Merlendi and I became more disturbed about the condition of the world. But most importantly, we were even more concerned about the condition of the church, or God's people. Where were the travailing women, the lamenting men, the priest that will weep between the porch and the altar for the souls of man? When will the church stand up and be the church that God is calling? What will it take for us, the people of God, to humble ourselves and pray, seek God, turn from our wicked ways so He will hear from heaven and heal the land? When will the leader/pastors lead the people back to God and prayer? We, the church, need to wake up from our slumber. We, the church, need to humble ourselves and pray before we can effectively pray for the world. We must get the fear of God back in us and back into our sanctuaries.

The LORD taketh pleasure in them that fear him, in those that hope in his mercy. — Psalm 147:11

And that, knowing the time, that now it is high time to awake out of sleep: for now is our salvation nearer than when we believed. — Romans 13:11

The last straw for us was on June 10th, 2016, when a young lady was murdered by a fan after her concert in Orlando, Florida. Two days later, in the wee hours of a Sunday morning on June 12th in Orlando, Florida, fifty people were massacred and fifty-three more wounded at a nightclub. Two days later, on June 14th, at a Disney Resort in Orlando, Florida, a little 2-year-old boy was snatched, take away and drowned by an alligator. These chains of events were devastating. It did not take a lot of discernment to see that something demonic was going on in Orlando. Merlendi and I could not understand that. A few hours after the nightclub shooting, that same Sunday morning, a few miles down the street from that nightclub, an Apostle/pastor/spiritual leader was having a birthday party and dancing in the sanctuary to some funk music.

We could not understand that at all. We are not perfect, but we figured now would be time for prayer and intercession. So much was happening. The young lady and many at the nightclub had lost their lives. Most likely, some were not saved, which means that they will sadly spend eternity in Hell. It is too late for those if they were not saved when they lost their lives, but then it would have been a good time to pray and try to snatch some of the other souls from the grip of the enemy that leads to eternal damnation. Some of the people were wounded and needed prayers for salvation and recovery. The little boy lost his life. The parents and a lot of people were crushed. The family of these people needed prayer. They needed God now more than ever before. Those that are called by the name of the Lord, our job is to pray for them. The church of God should have been thanking and praising because it could have been a whole lot more lives lost at that nightclub and those other places.

My daughter and I were heartbroken about what had transpired that we began to cry for God's people to get a continuous prayer chain moving. Prayer changes things and people. It brings revival and moves the hand of God. Prayer will cause God to step in and rebuke the enemy. If enough prayer warriors would come together, maybe not in person, but on social media or just in their homes, and each pick a time and commit to pray thirty minutes at that chosen time every day, we would see change. We would be pleasing God. If forty-eight prayer warriors would pick a time and commit to thirty minutes each day, that would cover the whole 24-hour day. But we felt that forty-eight prayer warriors would be hard to find to make that kind of commitment for the sake of souls and the sinful condition of the world.

My daughter and I felt the Lord was saying to us, "Then, you two pray." We felt that God was leading us to go on social media, namely Periscope and pray every day until He released us. We would rotate days, Merlendi would pray one day and I prayed the next. If one of us were busy and could not cover prayer on a particular day, then the other would cover each other, as long as there was prayer every day. The whole twenty-four hours would not be filled with prayer, but at least prayer each day would disrupt some of the dark plans of the enemy. We began the prayer on Periscope. Most times, we would not have but a few people on LIVE. Sometimes there would not be anyone else on but us, but we were obedient. It was not about the numbers. It was about releasing prayer into the atmosphere every single day over social media, and about obeying God. It was a sacrifice, but we committed and obeyed.

We met some other people hungry for God on social media. We continued everyday with prayer and some teachings as the Lord led. Except for two days, we were on for a whole year. Merlendi and I began on June 15th, 2016. We felt the release of the Lord on June 15th of 2017. It was not easy and a sacrifice, but a blessing as well.

We knew that along with intercession, there is bound to be spiritual warfare. We knew that God was covering us with His blood, but we needed to learn as much as we could about spiritual warfare. God was equipping us for the assignment. We would need to put on the whole armor of God.

[10] Finally, my brethren, be strong in the Lord, and in the power of his might.

[11] Put on the whole armour of God, that ye may be able to stand against the wiles of the devil.

[12] For we wrestle not against flesh and blood, but against principalities, against powers, against the rulers of the darkness of this world, against spiritual wickedness in high places.

[13] Wherefore take unto you the whole armour of God, that ye may be able to withstand in the evil day, and having done all, to stand.

[14] Stand therefore, having your loins girt about with truth, and having on the breastplate of righteousness;

[15] And your feet shod with the preparation of the gospel of peace;

[16] Above all, taking the shield of faith, wherewith ye shall be able to quench all the fiery darts of the wicked.

[17] And take the helmet of salvation, and the sword of the Spirit, which is the word of God: —Ephesians 6:10-17

We knew we needed to study, fast, and pray even more. We brought books on spiritual warfare, the prophetic, and prayer. We studied about how demons and evil spirits operate. We learned how to come against them always and only in the name of Jesus. The kingdom of darkness is highly organized; therefore, we must be very strategic. We never go after any spirit unless directed by God. We must stay in our spiritual jurisdiction. We are to rebuke only the demonic spirits that God leads us to. We are no match for the devil in our own strength, but only in the strength that God gives us, in Jesus' name.

I found that when studying God's Word, it will reveal to everyone the things in their lives that needed attention or be corrected. When we began to study spiritual warfare and deliverance, we discovered that there were things in our lives and family that needed attention. We learned about curses: cursed objects, generational curses, and ancestral curses. We gained knowledge on ways the enemy works and how he may have the legal right to work against us. Sometimes we may wonder why things happen in our lives, why we are not being blessed as we feel we should, or why things seem to be working against us. Cursed objects can cause demonic attacks and can hinder God's blessings.

Neither shalt thou bring an abomination into thine house, lest thou be a cursed thing like it: but thou shalt utterly detest it, and thou shalt utterly abhor it; for it is a cursed thing. — Deuteronomy 7:26

And ye, in any wise keep yourselves from the accursed thing, lest ye make yourselves accursed, when ye take of the accursed thing, and make the camp of Israel a curse, and trouble it. — Joshua 6:18

Merlendi had demonic attacks in her sleep for a while. The enemy would hold her down in her sleep and she could not move. Some may think that things such as that happen sometimes. But we should not accept anything that happens in our life without praying and seeking God for divine revelation. We should not be ignorant of Satan's devices. We had been praying against those sleep attacks and they seemed to subside. But after a few months, when we thought everything was fine, the attacks would happen again. Through our study about the spirit realm and things that could give the enemy the legal right to attack, we began to pray more intently and ask God to reveal whatever needed to be exposed. One day after an attack, God revealed to Merlendi an object in her home at the time. It was a cute little bird that had been sitting on her bed post for months. Birds can represent good or evil. We know that the eagle would be an example of good, representing the prophetic. The bird sitting on her bed was not for good. She destroyed it immediately.

We begin to go through both our apartments, praying and asking God to reveal whatever needed to be annihilated. We did not have things like skulls, occult objects, and things of that nature. But sometimes, beautiful keepsakes, souvenirs, and other items can be demonic that may seem alright. We destroyed so many things that God revealed to us that needed to be demolished. Even if we were not sure about certain things, we got rid of it anyway. We didn't want anything around or associated with us that was an abomination to God. We didn't want any hindrances to His blessings, or that would be a portal for the enemy to attack. We trashed certain books, pictures, souvenirs from different countries that deal with witchcraft, anything to do with the horoscope, stuffed animals, and objects that were revealed to us to remove from our home. We did a spiritual house cleaning. We repented for having anything of an accursed nature in our home.

We prayed to break generational curses. We repented for our ancestors of anything they may have done years before that would bring about a curse upon us. As we studied, we prayed and asked God to show us things that could be blocking certain blessings in our lives. As we studied and gained more knowledge, things began to take a turn in our lives. We begin to understand why certain things were the way that they were in our lives and family. When dealing with the spirit realm, especially the demonic realm, if we are not careful, the enemy will bring fear to try and stop us from gaining knowledge on how to break free of things that may have held us bound. We do not have to be anxious or live in fear of the enemy. Christ is our curse breaker. We come against the powers of darkness in the name of Jesus and by the power of His blood.

The LORD is longsuffering, and of great mercy, forgiving iniquity and transgression, and by no means clearing the guilty, visiting the iniquity of the fathers upon the children unto the third and fourth generation. — Numbers 14:18

Christ hath redeemed us from the curse of the law, being made a curse for us: for it is written, Cursed is every one that hangeth on a tree: — Galatians 3:13

We gained more wisdom and knowledge as we studied. The enemy does not want us to come into the knowledge of the truth. For us to grow in the ways of God, we must read His word and draw closer to Him. We also need to know about Satan's kingdom, so we can effectively wage war against him. God has made us watchmen, to watch and pray night and day until He hears and delivers His people.

[6] I have set watchmen upon thy walls, O Jerusalem, [which] shall never hold their peace day nor night: ye that make mention of the LORD, keep not silence,

[7] And give him no rest, till he establish, and till he make Jerusalem a praise in the earth. — Isaiah 62:6-7

Our original prayer time was 8 p.m. As we learned more about prayer and watches, we learned that there are eight prayer watches a day, beginning at 6 p.m. with the first watch. The third watch starts at 12 a.m.- 3 a.m., which is sometimes called the witching hour. This time is when the demonic activity is heightened because witches, warlocks, and Satanists are busy at work during this watch. The enemy operates during these hours because this when deep sleep falls upon us, and not a lot of people are praying at this time to offset and oppose Satan's activities.

¹⁵ In a dream, in a vision of the night, when deep sleep falleth upon men, in slumberings upon the bed;

¹⁶ Then he openeth the ears of men, and sealeth their instruction,

¹⁷ That he may withdraw man from his purpose, and hide pride from man.

¹⁸ He keepeth back his soul from the pit, and his life from perishing by the sword. — Job 33:15-18

Job 33:15-18 (Message Bible)
¹⁵⁻¹⁸ "In a dream, for instance, a vision at night,
when men and women are deep in sleep,
fast asleep in their beds—
God opens their ears
and impresses them with warnings
To turn them back from something bad they're planning,
from some reckless choice,
And keep them from an early grave,
from the river of no return

The 3rd watch is a time when the Lord speaks to us about things and maybe warns us of the adversary. Also, it is a time to pray against attacks on us, families, and even our nation. This watch is a very sacrificial time to wake up or stay up and pray. But God led us to this time, along with any other time the Holy Ghost leads us to pray. Of course, we are to read and study God's Word every day, and God will lead us to other materials to supplement our study. There are always books in bookstores and online materials. Some books and materials we find online are not of God. Therefore, we must pray and use our discernment as to which materials God wants us to study. The Holy Ghost will put a check in our spirit if it is something that He does not approve of us studying.

Study to shew thyself approved unto God, a workman that needeth not to be ashamed, rightly dividing the word of truth. — 2 Timothy 2:15

The more we study His Word, the more we know about Him, and the more faith we have in Him. Also, as we read the Bible, the more we know how the enemy works against us. We may have been praying about some situations for a long time. Even after praying, we may not have received an answer and wonder if God even hears us. But His Word tells us that we can be confident that whatever we pray according to His will, He hears us. God's Word is true. We walk by faith, not by what we see. What we see may be a deception planted by the enemy. God is not pleased if we do not have faith in Him. He will do what His Word says He will do, no matter how the enemy tries to bring fear in our minds that God did not hear our prayers, or if He heard, He will not answer. I have learned not to listen to anything contrary to what the Word of God says. God is pleased when we take Him at His Word and will answer in due season.

But without faith it is impossible to please him: for he that cometh to God must believe that he is, and that he is a rewarder of them that diligently seek him. — Hebrews 11:6

So then faith cometh by hearing, and hearing by the word of God. — Romans 10:17

And this is the confidence that we have in him, that, if we ask any thing according to his will, he heareth us: — 1 John 5:14

CHAPTER 7

ANOTHER PUSH

I wanted to get to know God in a deeper way and for Him to reveal mysteries unto me. We should never become satisfied and complacent with where we are in God. I strive for a higher dimension in Him. I want to see mighty breakthroughs in my life and others. I know that calls for a greater dedication to the Lord and the things of God. It also calls for a greater sacrifice. Some of us have no choice but to seek the deep things of God. That's why I can't be satisfied with the status quo, 'church as usual,' or a church program that programs God out. God wants to move mightily in our midst. Often, He is not allowed to come in the services in such a way that people leave changed. I had gotten so tired of seeing God's people come to church burdened and troubled. They have yokes and bondages, but they leave the same way they came. If we cannot get our burdens lifted at church, then where?

For us that want everything that God wants to give us, naturally and spiritually, we are tired of going to church and just getting entertained. We don't want to be entertained. We want to be delivered. We all have something that we need God to do or deliver us from. We need to hear the gospel preached with anointing, power, and then demonstration. We don't want to just hear a lot of songs being sung, with no anointing and no power. We are tired of just an encouraging message with no deliverance and freedom to follow. It's the anointing that destroys the yoke.

And it shall come to pass in that day, that his burden shall be taken away from off thy shoulder, and his yoke from off thy neck, and the yoke shall be destroyed because of the anointing. — Isaiah 10:27

God is a miracle worker, in every sense of the word. God wants to work miracles. I desire to see God do the miraculous in the sanctuaries. Too many people are hurting, bound by demons, sick, deep into sin, and sinking even deeper. Some may be almost ready to give up on God or life. Some are on their way to a burning hell. It is our job as the church, as God's people to reach these lost souls. We need God like never before. Now is no time to continue with the programs and entertainment. We need to see the hand of God in a mighty way.

The fear of God seems to have been lost in some churches. Almost anything goes. Some of the pastors/leaders seem to have lost the fear of God. They have sin in their lives, and it does not appear they are trying to repent and turn from their wicked ways. They tolerate sin in some of the people they are supposed to be leading to Christ and away from sin.

We as intercessors must pray that the pastors/leaders will wake up, and be the shepherds that God is calling for in these last and evil days. God wants His people to live holy lives and be an example for the world. We cannot do that if we are acting like the world. If we are prideful, sexually immoral, money hungry, covetous, and not living holy lives, we are displeasing to God. But God sees, and He will judge us that's called by His name if we continue in sin, and yes, God will judge, even the pastors/leaders.

¹¹ But now I have written unto you not to keep company, if any man that is called a brother be a fornicator, or covetous, or an idolator, or a railer, or a drunkard, or an extortioner; with such an one no not to eat.

¹² For what have I to do to judge them also that are without? do not ye judge them that are within?

¹³ But them that are without God judgeth. Therefore put away from among yourselves that wicked person. — 1 Corinthians 5:11-13

For the time is come that judgment must begin at the house of God: and if it first begin at us, what shall the end be of them that obey not the gospel of God? —1 Peter 4:17

When the Christians among us are committing sin and refuse to repent, Paul said in 1 Corinthians 5:11-13 that we should dissociate ourselves with them. We are not to even eat with them. That may sound harsh or uncaring, but not so, that's the word of God. I had to dissociate myself with some Christians, one being that former pastor/leader that refused to repent. I refuse to contaminate my walk with God by associating with unrepentant sinful Christians. I want the grace of God in my life. I will not offend God by keeping fellowship with any Christians, whether pastors/leaders or lay members, if they are living unholy lives. It's better to offend man than to offend God.

When the fear of God comes back into the church, repentance among God's people will take place. The fear of God will cause the people of God to turn from their wicked ways. The fear of God will cause the sinner man to give his life to the Lord. The fear of God motivates a man to repent. When the pastors/leader line their lives up with the Word of God, and they return to preaching the fear of God, more souls will be saved. Some pastors/leaders don't want to offend the church, so they don't preach the fear of God. They don't want their members to leave, or feeling condemned. Therefore they compromise. That is not the will of God to compromise the preaching of His Word to keep membership, or for any other reason. If pastors/leaders would obey God, stop watering down the sermons to make themselves and the congregation feel comfortable, and let the power of the Holy Ghost lead, lives will be changed, and then the church will grow.

Then had the churches rest throughout all Judaea and Galilee and Samaria, and were edified; and walking in the fear of the Lord, and in the comfort of the Holy Ghost, were multiplied. — Acts 9:31

For the past few years, I have been amazed and grieved how far some Christians have fallen away from holiness and righteousness. In my search for a church with a pastor/leader that is walking upright and living holy, I often wonder what happened and when did it happen? Why is the church in the state that it is in today? I wonder why some churches are not walking in the power that God intended. What is so different now from what took place in the early church? Why isn't the church seeing more miracles, signs, and wonders, and salvations? I believe the answer is sin. The Apostles in the book of Acts lived holy lives. They reverenced God. Their only agenda was God's agenda. They did not operate in pride, greed, sexual immorality, and self-centeredness. They were not worried about membership. They preached, taught the word of God with power, and cast out devils. It was the Lord that added to the church.

Praising God and having favour with all the people. And the Lord added to the church daily such as should be saved. — Acts 2:47

Not even as far back as the early Apostles, there were great men and women of God in the late 1800's and early 1900's. There were great revivals and moves of God that went down in history. How can we see the same in this day and time? I studied about some of those great revivalists from 100 to 150 years ago. Reading about the church meetings in those days made me even more hungry for God, miracles, signs, and wonders. The more I read, I found that most great moves of God began with living holy, prayer, and intercession. They had a passion for souls. They sacrificed their time and afflicted their bodies with prayer and fasting. I discovered that in this day and time, prayer seems to be a lost art in some churches and with Christians in general. It is sometimes hard to get people together for prayer meetings. I mean real prayer meetings, not a lot of talking, preaching, or teaching, but just calling on the name of Jesus. If we call on Him long enough, the miraculous is going to happen. Some don't want to pray any longer than a few minutes because they may get convicted of their sin because they have become comfortable in it. Some pastors/leaders and other people of God have seemingly gotten away with their sins for so long until they have become desensitized to the rebuke of God. If the people of God turn a deaf ear to God's correction, eventually He will turn them over to a reprobated mind. For some Christians, sinning becomes easier.

[28] And even as they did not like to retain God in their knowledge, God gave them over to a reprobate mind, to do those things which are not convenient;

[29] Being filled with all unrighteousness, fornication, wickedness, covetousness, maliciousness; full of envy, murder, debate, deceit, malignity; whisperers,

[30] Backbiters, haters of God, despiteful, proud, boasters, inventors of evil things, disobedient to parents,

[31] Without understanding, covenant breakers, without natural affection, implacable, unmerciful:

[32] Who knowing the judgment of God, that they which commit such things are worthy of death, not only do the same, but have pleasure in them that do them. —Romans 1:28-32

Romans 1:28-32 (Message Bible)

²⁸⁻³² Since they didn't bother to acknowledge God, God quit bothering them and let them run loose. And then all hell broke loose: rampant evil, grabbing and grasping, vicious backstabbing.

They made life hell on earth with their envy, wanton killing, bickering, and cheating. Look at them: mean-spirited, venomous, fork-tongued God-bashers. Bullies, swaggerers, insufferable windbags!

They keep inventing new ways of wrecking lives. They ditch their parents when they get in the way. Stupid, slimy, cruel, cold-blooded. And it's not as if they don't know better.

They know perfectly well they're spitting in God's face. And they don't care—worse, they hand out prizes to those who do the worst things best!

Being numb to sin is disheartening and so sad. Not only do some not rebuke sin, but they partake in it. How can God use us to win the lost, if some of us are living unholy lives and acting like sinners? It is our duty to be a light shining in the darkness. We are called to share the good news of the gospel. We might not be able to win every soul to Christ, but we should, for sure, be found trying. The early Apostles and even some of the revivalists were examples. They were set apart to be used by God. They endured many oppositions, yet they persevered. They did not live in big houses, drive the finest of cars, own planes, and their bank accounts weren't running over. There's nothing wrong with us as God's people enjoying the blessings of God, but when we love those things more than we love Him and doing His will, then that's a problem. Signs and wonders followed the early Apostles, and the power of God was demonstrated. Some people will not accept Christ unless they see or hear something to convince them that they need to come to Him. Where is the power in some of the churches today? What happened to holiness? Where is the love for

God for His people? How can we get back to where God wants us to be in our walk with Him? Repentance is the answer, but first, we must make up our minds to repent.

⁴ Nevertheless I have somewhat against thee, because thou hast left thy first love.
⁵ Remember therefore from whence thou art fallen, and repent, and do the first works; or else I will come unto thee quickly, and will remove thy candlestick out of his place, except thou repent. — Revelation 2:4-5

Revelation 2:4-5 (The Message)
⁴⁻⁵ "But you walked away from your first love—why? What's going on with you, anyway? Do you have any idea how far you've fallen? A Lucifer fall!
"Turn back! Recover your dear early love. No time to waste, for I'm well on my way to removing your light from the golden circle.

God is talking to one of the seven churches here in these Scriptures about how far they had fallen away from their love for Him and His people. Everything seemed alright on the outside. Much like today, there are mega churches, programs going on at church, the preacher may even be preaching, praise team singing, but God knows the real condition of the hearts. God was saying to the church at Ephesus, that if they did not turn back in a hurry, He was going to remove His light, presence, and glory from them. If God were to remove His light and His presence, then the church would just be an organization, going through the motions of church, but not a true church of Jesus Christ. That should bring fear back to the church and the people of God, causing them to get back in right standing with Him quickly.

Merlendi and I searched for a true move of God, where He is truly having His way. We attended so many church services looking for a place where God can move by His power without interruptions with the regular scheduled programs. Even some services, the preacher was preaching, praise team singing, shouting, giving offerings, going through the formalities, but in our spirit, we knew something was missing. We were streaming church services, watching YouTube sermons, and sermons on social media, but we were missing being a part of, not just a church, but a real move of God. We went to a prophetic conference being held by a prophet that we had seen on television. Since we are prophetic people, we were drawn to this type of atmosphere. At this conference, we received a word of knowledge from the prophet that was conducting the service. We learned some things through this word of knowledge that we did not understand before. Some things were happening in our lives that seemed to follow a pattern and could maybe be a stronghold. This man of God said that this pattern was a generational issue from my mother's house. He prayed for us so that the cycle would be broken off our lives, which caused Merlendi and I to delve deeper into studying about generational curses, bloodline curses, and spiritual warfare in general.

We had grown weary of searching for a ministry that deals in deliverance, and that allows God to do what He needs to do in the services to get the people delivered. We began to travel to conferences hosted by this man of God, even to other states in pursuit of the glory, and to try and find what the Lord was calling us to do. We needed to know what God was calling for us to do in this hour. We spent money on gas for vehicles, plane tickets, hotels, and food, trying to find what we needed spiritually. We were desperate for direction and the glory of God. At these conferences, we got to hear and be a part of different men and women of God's teachings and impartations. There were prophetic activations, deliverance teachings, and teaching about prayer. In the church today, we need the five-fold ministry alive and functioning. Because Merlendi and I have a prophetic calling on our lives, for years, we were not exposed to the teachings, and the prophetic was not activated in us.

¹¹ And he gave some, apostles; and some, prophets; and some, evangelists; and some, pastors and teachers;
¹² For the perfecting of the saints, for the work of the ministry, for the edifying of the body of Christ: — Ephesians 4:11-12

We endeavored to surround ourselves with these teachings and activations, even if we had to go to where it was being taught. We aimed to equip ourselves so that we may effectively do the ministry that God has called us to. We had received prophetic words over the years, but the prophetic was not being taught concerning prophetic prayers, prophetic declarations, and prophetic dreams.

Follow after charity, and desire spiritual gifts, but rather that ye may prophesy. — 1 Corinthians 14:1

We did not know that we should desire to prophesy until we began to attend these prophetic conferences and prophetic activations. After we were saved and filled with the Holy Ghost, we thought that prophecy was only for certain people in the body of Christ. Never did we know that we should desire to prophesy. I never understood why the enemy had fought me so long before I gave my life to Christ in the prophetic. I was once afraid of prophecy. I did not want to be around prophets. As I matured in the Lord, I understand that the enemy was trying to derail my destiny by causing fear to come upon me concerning prophets and prophecy. The body of Christ needs the prophetic operating in the church like never before. We all need to hear from God for ourselves, but many struggles in that area, therefore, receiving a prophetic word is vital to one's future. Just one word of prophecy can change the course or direction of a person's life. We found that just being in the company of prophets and other prophetic people stirred us to desire this gift even more. The Bible tells us that when Saul came into a company of prophets, he began to prophesy along with them.

And when they came thither to the hill, behold, a company of prophets met him; and the Spirit of God came upon him, and he prophesied among them. — 1 Samuel 10:10

Therefore, when we were around other prophets and prophetic people, we were not as fearful to speak the Word of the Lord. The apostle or prophet that was leading in the activations let us know that it was imperative to study and know the word of the Lord. They were not training us to prophesy. They were training us to listen and hear the voice of the Lord, and then release what we felt we heard. If we study the Bible, we can always give someone an encouraging word, or we can speak what the Word of God has already said concerning His people. Prophecy is one of the gifts of the spirit and God wants us to use that gift whenever He stirs us to.

[14] Neglect not the gift that is in thee, which was given thee by prophecy, with the laying on of the hands of the presbytery.
[15] Meditate upon these things; give thyself wholly to them; that thy profiting may appear to all. — 1 Timothy 4:14-15

I received a prophetic word from a brother concerning my living situation in the first prophetic activation that I was a part of. I lived in Texas at the time, but I had traveled to this prophetic activation, which was in another state, and I'm so glad I did. I did not know this brother that spoke the word of prophecy to me, nor did he know me, but he heard the voice of the Lord concerning my situation. During this time, I was living in a house that I had been in for over 17 years. The house was paid for, but for the last few years, it was in bad condition. It rained inside and needed major repairs. The house had roaches, mice, and other insects inside because there were holes in the walls. I did not have the finances to pay for repairs. The house had mold which spread to the household furniture. For about three or four winters, the house had no heat. I had to use a small electric heater in the bedroom and sleep under an electric blanket to keep warm. I stayed in bed most of the time in the winter to stay warm. I had a small air condition unit in the bedroom for the hot summer months. I was embarrassed for anyone to come over to visit. I did the best I could under those circumstances. I cried and felt sorry for myself. I waited for God to bless and work things out for me. I used to cry to God and remind Him that I had been faithful. I had given tithes and offerings in addition to thousands of dollars in ministries. I always give to people in need. I reminded God that I was living holy. I had decided to give God my all and had given Him a complete yes. It appears God did not hear my prayer, or if He did hear, He was taking a long time to deliver me from those conditions.

While at this prophetic activation, this gentleman told me that he heard God speak to him concerning my house situation. He said that the Lord said, "He was going to snatch me out of it." I received this prophecy in March, and I was so excited. A few days after I arrived back home, Merlendi came home for the weekend. She had been living in Dallas, Texas, ever since her graduation eight years earlier. I called and told her of the prophecy immediately after receiving it. She and I were in my bedroom in the house. I showed her how bad the closet was with mold where it had been raining. I had moved my clothes from that side of the closet, so they would not get wet. Merlendi told me that I should move out of this house, move into an apartment about 20 miles away, and sell the house. She had told me I should move out into an apartment a few years before this time, but I had paid for the home. I did not want to be responsible to pay the expensive rent on an apartment. When we have been praying and waiting for God to deliver us from certain situations, it can get frustrating when it seems that the deliverance will not come or is taking too long in coming. There are times when God has us in a waiting period, a wilderness season because He is birthing something in us and out of us. Then again, sometimes, when we think we are waiting for God, but He is waiting on us to hear His voice, have faith in Him and act on that faith, while trusting Him, no matter how things may appear.

Merlendi had spoken this to me a few years earlier, but at the time, it did not make good business sense to start paying rent when I had no mortgage to pay at this house. But the living conditions were horrible. I did not discern the voice of the Lord through Merlendi the first time she spoke to me concerning moving. God can speak in so many ways and through different people. But we must have an ear to hear what He is saying. This instance was where I needed discernment and I could have discerned that God was speaking through Merlendi a few years prior, telling me to move out of this house and not worry about the rent. In this situation, God's Word to me, did not fall on good ground. It fell among thorns and got choked out.

[3] And he spake many things unto them in parables, saying, Behold, a sower went forth to sow;

[4] And when he sowed, some seeds fell by the way side, and the fowls came and devoured them up:

[5] Some fell upon stony places, where they had not much earth: and forthwith they sprung up, because they had no deepness of earth:

[6] And when the sun was up, they were scorched; and because they had no root, they withered away.

[7] And some fell among thorns; and the thorns sprung up, and choked them:

[8] But other fell into good ground, and brought forth fruit, some an hundredfold, some sixtyfold, some thirtyfold.

[9] Who hath ears to hear, let him hear. — Matthew 13:3-9

I was single, but I was working at the time. God had blessed me to go through a nursing program and become a nurse. Still, I did not want to pay out almost a thousand dollars to rent an apartment every month. I was not thinking nor hearing clearly, because God had been trying to deliver me from the house situation for a few years, but my carnal mind, I missed it. He wanted me to have faith in Him. And faith without works is dead.

¹⁴ What doth it profit, my brethren, though a man say he hath faith, and have not works? can faith save him?

¹⁵ If a brother or sister be naked, and destitute of daily food,

¹⁶ And one of you say unto them, Depart in peace, be ye warmed and filled; notwithstanding ye give them not those things which are needful to the body; what doth it profit?

¹⁷ Even so faith, if it hath not works, is dead, being alone. — James 2:14-17

I thought I had faith in God, but I did not want to do the work required to go with it. After Merlendi and I talked about me moving out and selling the house, the word in me quickened. I saw the potential move differently. She also told me that she would make sure that my rent would be paid monthly. We began to look at apartments. I went the following week and filled out an application on a nice place she picked out. I got the apartment with no problems. I was so excited and thankful to God. I could hardly believe that I was leaving a bad situation with the house because I had been in it for so long. No matter how long we may have been dealing with a problem and it looks like deliverance won't come, it will happen.

I had gotten the prophetic word from the gentleman about God bringing me out of that situation in March. Less than two months later, on May 5th, I moved into this beautiful, large one-bedroom apartment. When I first got the key to the apartment, I opened the door, went in, and laid out on my face on the floor, thanking God for deliverance. You see, when the gentleman gave me the word of the Lord, and the second time Merlendi gave me the word of the Lord, it fell on good ground. I received it and it was bearing fruit. When God delivers us from adverse circumstances, whether it be a marriage, home conditions, controlling leaders, or whatever the case may be, it's amazing. The mind becomes at peace that's indescribable and our thinking is clear.

When I moved out of the house, I gave away so much. I gave furniture, new appliances, clothes, and other items. Merlendi and I are givers. We love to bless people and expect nothing in return, as long as God gets the glory. Even though the house was run down, the furniture and other things in the home were in good condition. I put the house up for sale. And within a few months, God had blessed me to sell it for more than I ever imagined. It's something about when we line up with God's will, be sensitive to His voice, then He opens the windows of heaven and pour us out blessings that we don't have room to receive.

That apartment was such a blessing and had been waiting on me to realize that God had better for me than the conditions I had been living in for quite a few years. God was waiting for me to realize that and have faith in Him. I used to walk through the apartment with my hands up, praising God. I would go out on the terrace in the wee hours of the morning, just looking around, looking up to heaven, and thanking God for His blessings. I was in awe of the Lord's blessings. I lived in that apartment for one year and seven months, and I never missed a rent payment. Neither was I ever late to pay. I never struggled to make a rent payment because Merlendi helped to make sure I was comfortable. The apartment was a little expensive, and I could have rented a cheaper one. But we get what we pay for. I paid for the neighborhood I wanted to live in. It was gated, beautiful, and I never had any trouble. The office managers were so nice and loved God. In addition, we had prayed as to where to move, and we felt God led us to this complex. God wanted me to have the best. He was giving me double for my shame. The blessings of the Lord come with no struggle.

The blessing of the LORD, it maketh rich, and he addeth no sorrow with it. — Proverbs 10:22

For your shame ye shall have double; — Isaiah 61:7

For all the shame and the anguish that I endured in that house I moved out of, God delivered me from there and made it up double with this apartment. Who am I to question God? After I moved into the apartment, I got up early every morning and drove to work. I would rush home in the evening to my new apartment. I was filled with joy and how God had delivered. I was no longer embarrassed to have guests come over. All the while I lived there, I would walk the entire complex and pray. I would pray for the other tenants as well. My closet was huge and that became my prayer closet. I even slept in it some nights. I could feel God moving in my life. I was invited to a church in this new town, and I went. The power and the presence of the Lord were present at the church. It was a prophetic ministry, and I knew wherever I attended or just visited, would need to be prophetic. Prayer and deliverance were a big part of this church. I attended for a few months and was blessed to work with the altar ministry of prayer and deliverance.

I am willing to work where God needs me. I do not mind laboring with people on the altar until they get their deliverance. I did not remain at the ministry long because I discerned that the leader may become controlling. I love church and worshipping God, but with work and other obligations, I was not willing to be in service most nights of the week, and on Sundays. I had recently been delivered from under a controlling pastor/leader and I did not want to run the risk of getting into a similar situation. I felt it best I not formally join this ministry, so I gracefully withdrew from the post I had been assigned.

So, Merlendi and I find ourselves yet again seeking God about ministry and what place we belonged. Where does God want us to serve in ministry? We were still traveling from state to state, attending the prophetic gatherings. We gained a lot of knowledge in classes on the deliverance ministry and prayer ministry that were offered. Men and women of God from all over the eastern United States and from other countries were preaching, teaching, and imparting in these conferences. We were chasing after a continuous move of God. We continued to watch teaching and preaching on social media as led by God. Not everything on social media is of God, and not everything is for everyone. We must use our spiritual discernment and rightly divide what we watch and what we hear. Even when receiving a prophetic word, the Bible tells us we are to judge prophecy and to beware because there are false prophets that come in sheep's clothing in the land. They may even be accurate, but what about their character and their aim.

Let the prophets speak two or three, and let the other judge. — 1 Corinthians 14:29

[13] Enter ye in at the strait gate: for wide is the gate, and broad is the way, that leadeth to destruction, and many there be which go in thereat:

[14] Because strait is the gate, and narrow is the way, which leadeth unto life, and few there be that find it.

[15] Beware of false prophets, which come to you in sheep's clothing, but inwardly they are ravening wolves.

¹⁶ Ye shall know them by their fruits. Do men gather grapes of thorns, or figs of thistles?

¹⁷ Even so every good tree bringeth forth good fruit; but a corrupt tree bringeth forth evil fruit.

¹⁸ A good tree cannot bring forth evil fruit, neither can a corrupt tree bring forth good fruit.

¹⁹ Every tree that bringeth not forth good fruit is hewn down, and cast into the fire.

²⁰ Wherefore by their fruits ye shall know them. — Matthew 7:13-20

Judge the prophetic word to see if it's biblical. Check out whether your spirit agrees with what is being said. Is the prophecy given to you in love and grace, rather than in anger and judgment? Don't be impressed with charisma; look for the character of the person. When I was receiving the prophetic words about God delivering me from my living situation at the time, I knew it was God. I did not know the gentleman that gave me the prophecy, but my spirit agreed with what he was releasing, and it came to pass. I know my daughter Merlendi, her character, and that she hears from God. But don't be deceived. There are false prophets out there that are cunning and will take advantage for their personal gain. Be prayerful and watchful.

We sought God through fasting and prayer concerning the direction in our lives. We did not have a spiritual leader with whom to seek Godly counsel. We only had each other to stand together in agreement. Merlendi and I felt that most people don't really understand the ministry that God entrusted us with. God has called and chosen us for a work in this end time, and we said a complete yes to Him. God has placed a burden for souls to be saved, delivered, healed and set free deep down in our spirits. All believers should have that burden. This is not to say by no means that Merlendi and I are the only two that God has put that burden inside. We see so many pastors/leaders, as well as other believers who compromise living holy lives, compromise people's deliverance and act like the world. Whether it's for fame, fortune, and status, God's Word, nor His will, should never be compromised. Merlendi and I will not compromise, nor will we conform to the way the world and a lot of churches are doing things, We will not settle for the status quo, nor for church, as usual. We will not be satisfied with an edited version of what God intended for His church to be. God's church should be a holy and with power.

And be not conformed to this world: but be ye transformed by the renewing of your mind, that ye may prove what is that good, and acceptable, and perfect, will of God. — Romans 12:2

We don't spend time trying to convince people of our relationship with God. We know that we seek to please God in everything that we do. Therefore, we trust God will lead and guide us into all truths. We try to eliminate as many distractions as possible to hear God clearly. We even refrained from watching television unless it's for spiritual edification. That's not to say that it's a sin to watch television, but we do have to guard our ear and eye gates. When we want to hear from God, we need to eliminate a lot of unnecessary noise. We need to know when God is speaking. When we want to hear the voice of God, we need to quiet our minds and our spirit and trust that He will speak. God tells us in His Word to trust Him, and not lean to our own understanding when we are seeking direction or whatever we need from Him.

[5] Trust in the LORD with all thine heart; and lean not unto thine own understanding.
[6] In all thy ways acknowledge him, and he shall direct thy paths.
—Proverbs 3:5-6

In seeking direction from God, we feel the Lord was leading us to move to another state, over 1000 miles away. Texas had been my home for 60 years and Merlendi had lived there for 28 years. We felt the leading of the Lord for us to move to Charlotte, N.C. We didn't know anyone in Charlotte. All our family and friends are in Texas. We just felt in our spirits that God was saying to move to Charlotte. We should never make major decisions on a prophetic word concerning a certain situation without seeking God diligently. First, we judge to see that the word is from the Lord. Next, we should pray for further instructions. It is of the utmost importance to move with and in God's timing. We should not move ahead of Him; neither should we linger too far behind His timing. Some instructions are time sensitive and need to be acted upon accordingly.

To move half-way across the United States was a gigantic step to make. We had heard there was going to be a move of God in Charlotte, North Carolina. Neither of us knew at that time, but great men and women of God have prophesied for years about a coming move of God in the Carolinas. We were excited, and we longed for a mighty move of God, a revival that will impact not only the place of its origin, but will spread to surrounding cities and states, and even the world; a revival that will leave people's lives forever changed. We are seeking for a move of God that will stir up the intercessors to begin to stand together in prayer, and that will bring to naught some of the evil that has been unleashed upon the earth. For example, murders, suicides, drugs, homosexuality, bullying, school shootings, church shootings, hot car deaths, strange happenings, and a host of other sins that are an abomination to our God.

We prayed about it for about six months. We did not have a problem with moving. We felt that we needed a change. We, as believers, should always be willing to go where God leads. We felt that we needed new surroundings, new territory, and fertile grounds so that some promises in our lives will begin to manifest. Even though God was blessing us, and He had done some amazing things in our lives, we still felt in our spirits that He wanted to do more. We both had some major prophecies that had been hanging over our heads for years, that had yet to come to past. We were grateful for all God's blessings, but He has provided some better things. We are expecting those things, not because we deserve them, but because His Word says we can have them.

God having provided some better thing for us, that they without us should not be made perfect. — Hebrews 11:40

We had recently learned that when someone receives a prophetic word, sometimes it does not automatically come to pass. For years, we were under the impression that when a prophetic word goes forth, we are to wait on it to manifest. Even with some of the promises in the word of God, there are times that we must work toward those promises. For example, if we give our tithes and offerings, then He will open the windows of heaven and other blessings.

[10] Bring ye all the tithes into the storehouse, that there may be meat in mine house, and prove me now herewith, saith the LORD of hosts, if I will not open you the windows of heaven, and pour you out a blessing, that there shall not be room enough to receive it.

[11] And I will rebuke the devourer for your sakes, and he shall not destroy the fruits of your ground; neither shall your vine cast her fruit before the time in the field, saith the LORD of hosts.

[12] And all nations shall call you blessed: for ye shall be a delightsome land, saith the LORD of hosts. —Malachi 3:10-12

Hence, some prophetic words that have been spoken over us may need to be prayed through until they manifest in our lives. Manifestations of some prophetic utterances, as well as promises in Scripture, sometimes could be held up because of demonic opposition. We were to learn later that when a prophetic word goes forth, then our adversary, the devil, also is privy to this information. When the word goes forth concerning our destiny, the enemy gets busy putting his demons on assignment to try and stop, block, or delay the manifestation of the prophecy. After this revelation, when a prophetic word is released to us, we immediately pray that the blood of Jesus covers that word. We pray that God will rebuke the hand of the enemy that would try and block the manifestation of that word.

We had faith that since we felt God was sending us to another state, the soil there will be fertile, and we expected to see miraculous changes in our circumstances as well as a mighty move of His Spirit. Our faith was telling us that whatever had been hindered and held up in Texas would be released through prayer and this move to North Carolina. During the months of praying concerning the move, never did we doubt that God was leading us in this direction. We both began preparations to move. Merlendi was finishing her nursing degree at the end of the six months, and that would be perfect timing to make the transition to North Carolina. We did not divulge any information to anyone of our intended move. No one, other than Merlendi and I knew of our plans until a couple of weeks before leaving. I gave my two-week notice on my job only two weeks before leaving. We decided not to share our plans with anyone, not even family. We should always keep our gifts hidden while they grow. We sometimes should not share what God is doing in our lives until the appropriate time. Not everyone will understand what God is doing in us. Not everyone will be happy for what God is doing in other's lives. Not everyone believes in forsaking all to follow Jesus. We were not going to chance anyone praying against our move. We were not giving the enemy any room to block or delay our relocation. We were reminded of when God told Abram to move from his kindred and go to where God was sending him. Abraham obeyed God and he and his seeds were blessed.

Now the LORD had said unto Abram, Get thee out of thy country, and from thy kindred, and from thy father's house, unto a land that I will shew thee: — Genesis 12:1

A couple of months before we were to move, we flew to Charlotte for an interview. On the plane heading to Charlotte, I felt really strange on the flight. I had flown before and had never felt that way. I can't sufficiently describe it, but it seemed as though I was losing control of my perception of what was going on around me. I felt that my breath was being taken away. I had no strength and felt that I was suffocating. I told Merlendi that I was not feeling well. Usually, on flights, we try to pray most of the time while airborne. But this time, we had to rely on the Holy Ghost to pray me through. Merlendi laid her hands on my back and she began to pray in tongues. I prayed as well as much as I could, but I felt stifled. We continued to pray in our heavenly language. The Bible tells us that when we pray in our heavenly language, it's the Holy Ghost making intercessions for us.

[26] Likewise the Spirit also helpeth our infirmities: for we know not what we should pray for as we ought: but the Spirit itself maketh intercession for us with groanings which cannot be uttered.
[27] And he that searcheth the hearts knoweth what is the mind of the Spirit, because he maketh intercession for the saints according to the will of God. — Romans 8:26-27

This was a time that I needed the Holy Ghost praying more than ever. We did not know what to pray for. We did not know what was going on. But the Holy Ghost knows all things. I don't know how long that episode lasted, but the Holy Ghost prayed us through it. Before we landed, I was back to myself. For a while, I did not know if I was going to make it through that situation. But thank God, I did. When we landed, we danced and praised God. We did not know at the time, but later the Lord showed us that the episode on the plane was a demonic attack and the enemy was upset about our move to North Carolina. But our God is a mighty deliverer. No matter what the enemy tries to throw our way, our God will shield us. He will hide us where the devil can't find us. Jesus' blood covers and protects.

CHAPTER 8

LED INTO A DESERT PLACE FOR DELIVERANCE

The job interview went well in North Carolina. We found a very nice apartment and the managers agreed to hold it until the day we set to return and move in. I felt great on the return flight. The hand of God had prevailed against the attack of the enemy on the going flight. Upon returning to Texas, we began packing and setting business matters in order before we were to move. Again, we blessed people with furniture, household items, and clothing from each of our apartments. We could have made a lot of money had we sold all the things that we gave to others. It wasn't that we didn't need the money. But we have found that it's more of a blessing to give than to receive. We did not charge anything. The Bible tells us that if we give, others will give to us.

I have shewed you all things, how that so labouring ye ought to support the weak, and to remember the words of the Lord Jesus, how he said, It is more blessed to give than to receive. — Acts 20:35

Give, and it shall be given unto you; good measure, pressed down, and shaken together, and running over, shall men give into your bosom. For with the same measure that ye mete withal it shall be measured to you again. — Luke 6:38

We shipped everything that we did not give away, except items that would fit in our vehicles. Both vehicles were loaded to the maximum. We drove because we did not want to ship either vehicle. We begin our journey on a Monday morning and it was raining. It rained so badly that we spent a night in three different states and did not arrive in Charlotte until the following Thursday morning. It was a long, rainy, and tiresome trip. We prayed most of the way. The word tells us that God gives His angels charge to keep us safe.

For he shall give his angels charge over thee, to keep thee in all thy ways. — Psalms 91:11

We were determined to begin this new chapter in our lives. We were excited to see what this new chapter holds for us. We trusted that God's hand was upon this move and He would keep us safe. We moved into the apartment as expected and prayed that God would manifest Himself in a mighty way in our lives and give us further instructions concerning His will. We continued in our midnight prayer, as well as whenever we were prompted to pray, praise, and worship. We had no family or friends here in North Carolina. We had each other and God is always with us.

Ironically, the host of the prophetic conferences that we traveled to attend when we lived in Texas was pastoring a church in Charlotte. He was the same prophet that gave us a word of knowledge concerning some generational issued that had been in our bloodline a year and a half earlier. We decided to attend some of the services to see what God may be saying concerning us fellowshipping with this church, also to get the generational issue addressed and broken if needed. We were apprehensive about going because, for one thing, when we were first drawn to follow this prophet, the glory of the Lord was present in a powerful way in the services. But, as time went on, it appeared that the visitation of the glory was censored or edited. Even after we noticed that the services were not how they had been in the beginning, we continued to attend. Another reason we were apprehensive about attending is because this prophet had charisma, but in our opinion, he did not possess good character. 1 Timothy 3 tells us the attributes that a pastor should possess. He should be above reproach, not prideful or greedy, as well as some other traits. This prophet was arrogant, prideful, and manipulative, in our opinion. He could preach, sing, and prophesy. He was accurate with most of his prophecies, but his character was very distasteful.

Once again, to give some understanding, I take no pleasure in revealing these things concerning a pastor's/prophet's character, but I do speak the truth. So why did we continue to attend this prophet's services? One reason is that since he had given us the word of knowledge back in Texas. He told us that he was going to break a generational stronghold off our bloodline. We trusted that it was broken because we trusted his voice at that time. Another reason is that for over a year, I had been seeing him in my dreams. Most of the dreams were spiritual. To be clear, I had no underlying romantic, sexual fantasies, or desires for this man of God. So that would not be a basis for any dreams concerning him. In some biblical dream interpretation books, to have a prophet show up in a dream usually means they represent God or some spiritual authority, maybe even that he's bringing a message. I had no one I could talk to that would help with the interpretations of those dreams. Therefore, my interpretation was that maybe this prophet was somehow connected to some deliverance that my bloodline needed.

We feel that prophets walk in the authority to break strongholds, curses, and bondages off people's lives, or rather they should.

Truthfully, if it were not for the dreams, I was having of him, we would have stopped following him months before. We feel that he hears from God, and we usually went to his meetings fasting and praying that God would show him whatever he needed to see concerning our situation since he is a seer. A seer is someone with supernatural insight. But each time we went, he never addressed our concerns. We weren't sure, but maybe God was not showing him anything yet, so we continued to hope for the next time.

Now here in North Carolina, we felt that we should visit his church to see if we could get some questions answers. The church was about 45 minutes away. We began to fast and pray before going and in route to the services. We made the trip every Sunday night. We prayed that God would reveal the meaning of me having dreams with the prophet in them. After almost every service, we were disappointed that we did not get what we needed out of the service. God is concerned with every aspect of our lives. God wants us delivered, healed, and set free. We feel that if God could truly have His way in our services, the glory will come in so thick that every situation will be addressed.

We had been praying about what steps we should take as far as becoming connected to this ministry. We felt that some breakthroughs might be for the people that are in covenant with the house. We really did not have a clear answer from God yet, but we did not feel God was opposed to us joining either. We are not people that go from one ministry to the other because of something we didn't like, but should we decide to connect, we could always disconnect if it was not in God's will. We also felt that this pastor/prophet was controlling, manipulative, and dominating, which means charismatic witchcraft once again. We thought that he manipulates the people into giving large sums of money in a cunning way, which is what our spiritual discernment showed us while attending his prior meetings. We knew what to anticipate and how to act accordingly.

I decided and initiated the step towards us joining this prophet's church. Even Merlendi didn't understand why I made the decision. I explained to her that we know how to protect ourselves and not be manipulated. We were only going to give in offerings as led by God. I felt we should take this step to cover every angle that could lead us to breakthrough. After we became a member of the house, we had some rights, whereas, if we were only visitors, we had none as far as covenant goes. We joined this ministry with caution. We kept hoping every Sunday, as well as attending Bible study on Tuesday nights, that the prophet would hear from God. Or if he was already hearing, then he would let us know if we needed deliverance and if that deliverance was going to come through him. Either way, I needed to understand why I had been seeing him in my dreams. A short while after we moved, I stopped having the dreams as frequently. I only had maybe one or two dreams with the prophet in them since we moved and joined the church. We were faithful to attending services and bible study weekly. We must admit that even though we prayed and interceded for the service on the way to the church when we left, we did not feel we had been helped in the area we needed the most help. The enemy had begun to attack Merlendi in her dreams and we needed more than just an encouraging message.

One night a couple of months after we arrived in Charlotte, Merlendi woke up from her sleep. She had no strength and was literally on the floor, limp. I heard her and went in to see what the problem was. She could hardly say anything, but she voiced that she was nauseous, had severe abdominal pain and heart palpitations. She felt as if all her strength was gone and thought she was going to pass out. At one point, all she could say was "Jesus." I began to pray and command Satan in the name of Jesus to take his hand off her. Looking at her, it appears her breath was leaving her. I was beyond scared and began praying in my heavenly language. While she was on the floor and I was trying to figure out whether to call 911 or to carry her to the hospital myself. The God of heaven revealed to me this was a demonic attack. Indeed, the enemy wanted to snatch her life. He wanted to see her graveyard dead. But the Lord revealed that she shall live and not die, to declare the works of the Lord. The enemy desires to see some of you that are reading this book dead as well. But in accordance to Psalm 118:17, you shall live and not die and declare the works of the Lord. John 10:10 lets us know that the thief cometh not, but for to steal, and to kill, and to destroy: I am come that they might have life, and that they might have it more abundantly.

I got consolation, knowing that she was going to make it out of this alive. Somehow, I got her downstairs into the car. I drove her to the nearest hospital, which was about 10 minutes away. By the time we got to the emergency room, she had said, "I am not going in." I looked at her and I knew whatever had attacked her had been rebuked. That let us know that the attack was indeed a spiritual one from the enemy. Her strength was beginning to return to her. We drove back home, thanking God for deliverance.

After she rested a bit, she told me that the attack began in her sleep where she encountered an incubus spirit. Incubus is an evil spirit that has sexual intercourse with women while they are sleeping. Since we had been studying spiritual warfare and how the enemy operates in the spirit realm, we understood and knew how to discern and begin to pray against those spirits. This attack was on a Sunday morning and even though this attack had left her drained, Merlendi decided to go to church that Sunday night. We went to this church hoping that the prophet, our pastor/spiritual leader at the time, would discern what was going on with her in the service and she would get some deliverance. That did not happen. The church service went on as usual, and no altar call for prayer that could bring her deliverance from any future attacks. We left discouraged. The attacks continued periodically for about three months. Each time the incubus spirit would attack her, we would always pray and challenge that foul spirit. We continued to go to church every week and the prophet did not discern what was going on or if he did, there was no altar call for prayer against demons attacking. God's people should not go to church bound and leave bound. Deliverance should be made available to anyone that is seeking it.

Merlendi and I decided that since we were going to church and neither of us were getting what we needed to get a council meeting with the prophet, who was our pastor. We had the administrative pastor's email, so we decided to email him to ask if we could get a meeting because we needed counseling in some areas. The assistant pastor emailed us back and asked what we needed to discuss with the prophet so that he could relay the message. We told him that Merlendi was being attacked in her sleep and we needed some assistance in breaking the attacks. Also, we wanted to get some understanding of why we had been planting large seeds into the prophet's ministry while we followed his conferences and we had not received a harvest yet after a couple of years. We understand that some harvests take time, but this prophet often stated that those who sowed would reap a harvest within a specified time frame. If they did not reap a harvest within that time frame, he promised to return the seed. Unfortunately, that did not happen. Merlendi and I waited to see if we would be granted a meeting. The administrative pastor informed us that this information would be relayed to the prophet. For several weeks, we waited to hear from the prophet regarding these matters.

Let me explain why we wanted to speak with the prophet versus the administrative pastor. We reverence all members of the five-fold ministers. However, prophets have the unique ability to see what others cannot see. Prophets can discern what others cannot discern. Some prophets are anointed to break yokes and fetters. At the time, the issues that Merlendi and I were facing needed the assistance of a prophet. Since we followed and wholeheartedly supported this prophet, we felt as though we needed to meet with him. Unfortunately, the prophet never responded to our request for a meeting, neither through email, nor did he talk with us one on one. We feel he did get the message via the administrative pastor because he made some comments from the pulpit that led us to believe he may have been referencing us. The comments were mocking and were not made in love, in our opinion. We were hurt and knew we could not continue attending this church every Sunday expecting breakthrough and leaving empty-handed. God is the author of peace and not confusion. At this point, we had no choice but to withdraw our membership and seek the Lord to deliver us and heal that hurt. We sent an email to the administrative pastor, informing him that we would be withdrawing our membership. Also, even though they never asked for forgiveness, we stated in the email that we forgive him and the prophet for how we were mistreated. There will undoubtedly be a time in our lives when people may have wronged us, and they may never ask us to forgive them. We must forgive them anyway and let God right the wrong. The forgiveness is for the person that was mistreated more than for the person that did the mistreating.

I speak now, from a place of deliverance. However, it did not automatically happen just because I'm saved and a Holy Ghost filled believer. It was a process. After we withdrew our membership and distanced ourselves from that ministry, it took prayer and giving the situations to God before we felt delivered. We had to pray because we did not want unforgiveness, bitterness, anger, and strife to set up in our hearts. No man is worth our salvation and our peace of mind. We will let nothing or no one to separate us from the love of God. After this prophet mishandled Merlendi and me, we did not want to see any pictures of him on social media and hear any CDs by him. We had a prayer CD by him that we had previously listened to faithfully. After we were offended by this prophet, we discarded it. There was nothing wrong with the prayer on the cd itself. Even though we respected the office of the prophet that he held, we did not appreciate that he mistreated us. We gave all the t-shirts that had his name on them that we had purchased from his ministry to Goodwill. Our actions were not out of anger. It was out of hurt, shame, offense, and disbelief that a shepherd, a man of God, could show blatant disrespect for God's people by not attempting to walk them through deliverance or give understanding where they were confused. Especially, when we had specifically informed his administrative pastor why we were asking for a meeting with the prophet/our spiritual leader at the time.

All we were asking that he pray and uproot any demonic spirits that were attacking Merlendi in her sleep. We had waited for weeks while attending the services for deliverance to come while in the prayer or worship, but it had not happened. We had prayed and waited for him to see and discern the attacks. So, maybe he could allow the glory of God to linger in the service until deliverance took place, not only for Merlendi but for others that needed deliverance. We just requested him to give us godly counsel and give us understanding from a godly standpoint. We needed him to let us know if he saw any demonic opposition that was blocking any of our deliverance or our blessings. That is what a shepherd is commissioned by God to do. Jesus is concerned about all the sheep. Jesus is the good shepherd and he left the ninety-nine to look for the one that had strayed.

[12] How think ye? if a man has an hundred sheep, and one of them be gone astray, doth he not leave the ninety and nine, and goeth into the mountains, and seeketh that which is gone astray?

[13] And if so be that he find it, verily I say unto you, he rejoiceth more of that sheep, than of the ninety and nine which went not astray.

[14] Even so it is not the will of your Father which is in heaven, that one of these little ones should perish. — Matthew 18:12-14

We were not asking for any finances from him. We were confused and needed his counsel. We were entitled because we were under his leadership, and in covenant with the house. The reason I had joined this ministry with apprehension was now revealed. If we had not been a member and under his leadership, we probably would not have been upset, nor would we have felt entitled to counsel. But since we were members, we feel counsel is a part of what leaders should do. We rendered tithes, offerings, and we supported financially in the previous conferences that we attended that this prophet hosted. We only desired maybe fifteen minutes of his time. Even had we not received a meeting, we felt at the least, we were worthy of an email or letter from him giving us understanding. We have since repented to God for not wanting to see him on social media, discarding his prayer CD, and giving the shirts to Goodwill. We repented because we were reacting to the offense we felt in our hearts. We did not want to hold onto anything, tangible or intangible, that would keep us in alignment with this man of God's spirit. We prayed and asked forgiveness, then fell out of alignment with him after being under his leadership. We also prayed to break any word curses that may have been spoken by him concerning us after withdrawing membership from his ministry. God's people should not be ignorant of the fact some pastors/spiritual leaders will speak word curses, knowingly or unknowingly against anyone that leaves their ministry. Of course, this is not of God, but some do it, nonetheless.

After we repented, God delivered us because He knows our hearts. We now hold no grudges nor unforgiveness in our hearts. God gave us the grace to quickly line up with His will and give the situation to Him. We began to pray for this prophet earnestly. It was hard in the beginning to ask God to bless him after we felt as though he had abused us. But we got there. We kept praying and God lifted the offense out of our hearts. Now we feel the love of God for the prophet.

If he needed us in any way, we will be there to help. We are not to seek revenge. God will vindicate His people that been mistreated.

[19] Dearly beloved, avenge not yourselves, but rather give place unto wrath: for it is written, Vengeance is mine; I will repay, saith the Lord.

[20] Therefore if thine enemy hunger, feed him; if he thirst, give him drink: for in so doing thou shalt heap coals of fire on his head. —Romans 12:19-20

It seems to be a hard thing for a man of God to admit that he has mistreated people and that they need deliverance. When a pastor/leader is not delivered themselves and has pride, control issues, arrogance, rejection, and offenses in their lives, they sometimes tend to minister from a wounded and an undelivered place. That is not healthy for them, nor for the people that sit under their leadership. These pastors/leaders may also cause the people to stumble that are assigned to lead. The Bible is clear that God is not pleased with pastors that scatter the sheep.

[1] Woe be unto the pastors that destroy and scatter the sheep of my pasture! saith the LORD.

[2] Therefore thus saith the LORD God of Israel against the pastors that feed my people; Ye have scattered my flock, and driven them away, and have not visited them: behold, I will visit upon you the evil of your doings, saith the LORD.

[3] And I will gather the remnant of my flock out of all countries whither I have driven them, and will bring them again to their folds; and they shall be fruitful and increase.

[4]. And I will set up shepherds over them which shall feed them: and they shall fear no more, nor be dismayed, neither shall they be lacking, saith the LORD. — Jeremiah 23:1-4

Hopefully, by sharing how these men of God have wronged us, other believers will know how to protect themselves from making the same mistakes we made. Merlendi and I consulted the Lord as to why He led us from Texas to North Carolina when seemingly more job opportunities were back in Texas, and we were already established there. I must confess that we began to get a little weary because things were not happening as we anticipated when we first arrived in Charlotte. We even began to question if we heard God correctly as to us moving to North Carolina. But God tells us not to get weary in well-doing.

And let us not be weary in well doing: for in due season we shall reap, if we faint not. — Galatians 6:9

We decided to stand in faith about what we believe. We believed we were led and directed by God to make this move and we were going to have to see it through. Those incubus attacks continued to plague Merlendi in her sleep for a few months. They were so bad at one time that she was afraid to go to sleep for fear of an attack. We studied and prayed warfare prayers to break that demonic spirit. We walked the floor as we prayed and pleaded the blood of Jesus. We tried to discern whether the enemy had any legal right to attack Merlendi. Whatever God showed us, we prayed accordingly. We do not have to stay bound by the enemy. We belong to God and He wants His people free. God has given us power over all the power of the enemy.

Behold, I give unto you power to tread on serpents and scorpions, and over all the power of the enemy: and nothing shall by any means hurt you. — Luke 10:19

Merlendi began to pray Scriptures on peaceful sleep and divine protection before she went to bed every night. She even prayed the Scriptures before naps because the attacks were so severe.

I will both lay me down in peace, and sleep: for thou, LORD, only makest me dwell in safety. — Psalm 4:8

When an attack awakened her, she always challenged it. She did not just go back to sleep. She would get up, walk the floor, and rebuke the enemy. She rebuked and canceled anything that the enemy may have tried to implant within her during the attacks. After a few weeks, we noticed that the attacks begin to lose their strength as she prayed and rebuked that spirit. She began to do warfare, even in her sleep. While she slept, God gave her the discernment that the enemy was trying to attack, and she would rebuke it while asleep to keep it from manifesting. Merlendi labored in prayer until God delivered her from those demonic spirits and gave her authority over them in Jesus' name. God gets the glory; no man gets the glory for walking Merlendi through deliverance from those attacks. God, by His Holy Spirit, gave her power and authority. Her testimony will break others free from those demonic bondages.

A short time after the attacks were canceled, we took a six-week class on spiritual warfare. Through those classes, we learned that often when someone, especially an intercessor, goes into a region, the enemy of that region will try and attack them. The attack could possibly be by the demonic spirits that thrive in that area. After this revelation, I was reminded of the demonic attack on my life on the flight to North Carolina. It appears that the enemy did not want us in this territory. Through these attacks, we even understood more of our assignment in North Carolina. Part of our assignment is strong intercession. Since arriving in North Carolina, we were led to pray as we ride through the streets. As children of God, we are always being delivered, and rather we should be. For instance, after we have been delivered from fornication, we may need deliverance from bitterness or some other issues. The enemy is never going to leave us alone. The Bible tells us that the devil is always seeking to devour us.

Be sober, be vigilant, because your adversary the devil walketh about as a roaring lion, seeking whom he may devour. — 1 Peter 5:8

Though we had gotten confirmation in our prayer time with the Lord that we were sent to this region to help pray and usher in a move of God, we still found ourselves becoming weary because some things were yet to come into fruition. God tells us in His word not to get weary in well-doing because we will reap if we don't faint. We had to learn to wait on God. God moves in His own timing. Had we not known that God had chosen us for this assignment, we would have fainted. We knew we could not move back to Texas until our assignment was completed. It is a huge task and called for a great sacrifice.

[13] I had fainted, unless I had believed to see the goodness of the LORD in the land of the living.
[14] Wait on the LORD: be of good courage, and he shall strengthen thine heart: wait, I say, on the LORD. — Psalm 27:13-14

We had to learn how to not only wait on God but to be of good courage while we do it. God does not want us murmuring and complaining like the children of Israel did. Murmuring caused the children of Israel great consequences. God had some many miracles for them, yet they complained. God has done so many great things for Merlendi and I. We sinned against Him by complaining about how we felt things would be different and better here in North Carolina. God did not want us thinking we would rather be back in Texas than here in North Carolina. God let us know that He was displeased with our impatience. We complained about the expenses incurred because of this move. We felt disillusioned because we had yet to find a church that fosters a move of God. With all the discontentment, we were fighting against the will of God for our lives. We heard a message that grumbling attacks God's sovereignty. God wants us to trust Him because He knows what's best. After we listened to this message, we immediately repented to God for complaining and not trusting Him completely. We felt so remorseful that we allowed ourselves to look back because when we do that, we take our eyes off God. We decided not to resist what God was doing and how He was doing it in our lives. We began to align ourselves with His will. God always has a plan for our lives.

[11] For I know the thoughts that I think toward you, saith the LORD, thoughts of peace, and not of evil, to give you an expected end.
[12] Then shall ye call upon me, and ye shall go and pray unto me, and I will hearken unto you.
[13] And ye shall seek me, and find me, when ye shall search for me with all your heart. — Jeremiah 29:11-13

Soon after we got our minds back on God's purpose for our lives and what He called us to do, things begin to shift in the spirit realm. We felt some opposition was broken. Things started to turn in our favor. We began to understand that it is a great honor that God chose the two of us for such an assignment as leaving everything we know and move to a place so far away. He could have chosen two other people that would not have complained, but God was merciful towards us. We know we are not the only people that God has moved to other parts of the country or world for kingdom assignments. Some others have the testimony that God told them to leave their hometowns and move here to Charlotte. We started to feel such peace that God is navigating our every move. God began to do some amazing things on our behalf. God keeps reminding us that we cannot settle for less than what He has for us in every area of our lives. We are hungry for Him and His righteousness. The Bible lets us know that we are blessed because we are hungry and thirsty for the things of God, and we will be filled. We are hungry for a mighty move of God.

Blessed are they which do hunger and thirst after righteousness: for they shall be filled. — Matthew 5:6

Where there is a demand for more of God, there is also an abundant supply. God has a set time for the unquenchable fires of the Holy Ghost to be ignited. Meanwhile, we are to do what we were sent here to do. We are going to gain much more than we feel like we may have lost by moving here. We learned how to be content. We seek the Lord diligently by fasting, praying, and reading His Word. We watch respected men and women of God teach the word of God online. We stay saturated with praise and worship. We spend time sitting in the presence of God. We listen for His leading and direction. We must not get in a hurry and do things in our own strength. God always has a set time for everything.

For everything there is a season, and a time for every matter under heaven: — Ecclesiastes 3:1

Though we met some disappointments upon arriving in Charlotte, God will use every little disappointment to catapult us into our purpose. The demonic oppositions we encountered when we moved here is working for our good. Having been misused and abused by the prophet/pastor after we arrived here will also work for our good.

And we know that all things work together for good to them that love God, to them who are the called according to his purpose. — Romans 8:28

God has a purpose. Once we became submitted to His will, we began to see His hand move on our behalf. As we humbled ourselves and fully surrendered to His purpose, we experienced a peace that surpasses all understanding. After God delivered us from whining and complaining, we started to see the manifestation of natural and spiritual blessings. We learned how to be content and trust God that He knows what's best and that we belong to Him. God has spared my life so many times, for which I'm forever grateful. Therefore, whatever His will is for my life, then His will be done.

Notwithstanding, the labor pains leading up to deliverance cannot compare to the breakthrough that's about to be achieved. The labor pains become more frequent and intense, leading up to natural delivery. Sometimes the mother may even feel as though she can't make it through. But after the baby is delivered, the joy outweighs the pain. As it is with spiritual labor pains that lead up to deliverance, we may feel that we cannot make it out of whatever uncomfortable situation we may find ourselves in at a given time. But God is there guiding us through the process. Whether our sins or mistakes, someone else, or life itself that caused the pain, the deliverance we obtain should surely bring us closer to God. God is birthing something out of us via afflictions. The afflictions build character, trust, and a deeper love for God. God uses our circumstances to glorify and show Himself strong.

[17] The righteous cry, and the LORD heareth, and delivereth them out of all their troubles.
[19] Many are the afflictions of the righteous: but the LORD delivereth him out of them all. — Psalm 34:17,19

I have to say that I've had more than a fair share of afflictions but a lot more deliverances. We never get past being afflicted because the Bible tells us that they are many. They are a part of life. Even when we try to do good, evil is always present. Many times, my aim and desire were to do good, but evil was there trying to overthrow me, trying to get me to give up on living for God. But giving up is not an option. I have come too far and suffered too many afflictions to give up. For most of my childhood, I was not happy. I had no choice as to how my childhood played itself out, but leaving home was my deliverance. Also, for most of my first marriage, I was miserable. Looking back, I did have a choice, but I chose to align myself with the control, domination, and abuse at the hands of my ex-husband. Then, most of my life in the streets, there was no real happiness. I chose to align myself with drugs and other sinful behaviors. At the age of 35, I accepted Christ as my Lord and Savior, who was my deliverance in that situation. I feel that a void was filled, as I began a new life. I thought I was leaving all the shame, domination, and control behind me.

But here it is over twenty years after accepting Christ, and I find that I had yet again aligned and allowed myself to be dominated, manipulated, and controlled by my then pastor. For years, I did not know this type of control is called charismatic witchcraft. Others had warned me that I was getting myself into an unfavorable situation, but I would not listen. I made excuses for my behavior. It is hard to convince someone they are being manipulated while they are under the manipulator's control. The manipulator was a man of God; therefore, I conformed and came into agreement with the manipulation. I made this person an idol because even when the Lord opened my eyes to this behavior, I did not remove myself from the situation until years later. Then fast-forward a couple of years, I once again aligned myself with manipulation and domination with another spiritual leader. I should have known better, but with this last manipulation, I was in pursuit of God. It is no excuse, by far, but this time I can truthfully say that after repenting for the alignments, I am delivered. By the grace of God, I will never allow myself ever to be dominated or controlled again by anyone.

I have reiterated these struggles that I have experienced to uncover the subtle and dangerous spirit of manipulation, domination, and control. That spirit is sneaky, especially when it comes to the spiritual arena. If we are not careful, we will feel as though we are obeying God by being submissive to controlling leaders. That is not true because the opposite is. Witchcraft is a spirit that God is adamantly against. If we align ourselves with it, whether knowingly or unknowingly, we are sinning against ourselves and God.

[19] Now the works of the flesh are manifest, which are these; Adultery, fornication, uncleanness, lasciviousness,

[20] Idolatry, witchcraft, hatred, variance, emulations, wrath, strife, seditions, heresies,

[21] Envyings, murders, drunkenness, revellings, and such like: of the which I tell you before, as I have also told you in time past, that they which do such things shall not inherit the kingdom of God. — Galatians 5:19-21

This spirit must be exposed, decoded, and destroyed by the power of the blood of Jesus. How do we expose spiritual leaders operating in witchcraft? We refuse to keep quiet any longer. Some of us are afraid that we are 'touching' God's anointed or that we are wrong if we speak out. That's one reason this spirit has been able to thrive in the church for so long. God is not in agreement with sin, whether the pastor is committing it or anyone else. Pray and be led by God as to how He would have the sin be exposed. God wants us always to do things descent and in order.

When a woman has been through childbirth for a few times and delivered children, she can subsequently help other women with the knowledge she has gained. Similarly, those who have been through many different afflictions, troubles, and deliverances on this Christian journey are expected to help others try to avoid as many pitfalls as possible. God is not pleased if we keep quiet, knowing that our brother or sister needs to be warned of possible impending affliction or iniquities.

But if the watchman see the sword come, and blow not the trumpet, and the people be not warned; if the sword come, and take any person from among them, he is taken away in his iniquity; but his blood will I require at the watchman's hand. — Ezekiel 33:6

We are our brother's keeper. We should do what's in our power to enlighten them, so they won't suffer some of the things we endured. Deliverance is an ongoing process. After we make up in our minds to yield our lives to the Lord, there is a plan of salvation and being born again. First, we must acknowledge God is the Creator of us and all things. Next, we must realize that we are sinners and we need God. We must believe that Jesus is the Son of God and that He sent His son to die for our sins.

For God so loved the world, that he gave his only begotten Son, that whosoever believeth in him should not perish, but have everlasting life. — John 3:16

We must believe that Jesus died on the cross for our sins, but He rose on the third day with all power and is seated at the right hand of the Father in Heaven. We must also repent and ask God to forgive us for all our sins for rejecting Christ. After repentance, we must accept God's forgiveness. We confess with our mouth and believe in our hearts unto salvation.

[9] That if thou shalt confess with thy mouth the Lord Jesus, and shalt believe in thine heart that God hath raised him from the dead, thou shalt be saved.

¹⁰ For with the heart man believeth unto righteousness; and with the mouth confession is made unto salvation. — Romans 10:9-10

There are several reasons to accept our Lord Jesus as our personal Savior. I feel that ultimately the two of the most crucial reasons are:
1. Just because of who He is.
2. After this life is over, we must spend eternity somewhere.

There are only two choices, either we accept Christ as our personal Savior and spend eternity in heaven with our Lord, or we reject Him and spend eternity burning in hell, which is forever torment.

He that believeth on the Son hath everlasting life: and he that believeth not the Son shall not see life; but the wrath of God abideth on him. — John 3:36

And shall cast them into a furnace of fire: there shall be wailing and gnashing of teeth. — Matthew 13:42

Then shall he say also unto them on the left hand, Depart from me, ye cursed, into everlasting fire, prepared for the devil and his angels: — Matthew 25:41

⁸ In flaming fire taking vengeance on them that know not God, and that obey not the gospel of our Lord Jesus Christ:
⁹ Who shall be punished with everlasting destruction from the presence of the Lord, and from the glory of his power; — 2 Thessalonians 1:8-9

Looking back, we can see our mistakes and what we should have done differently. We aim not to sin against God. How-be-ever, we will sin and fall, but we don't have to remain in sin. We should confess our sins, repent, and turn from them. God does not want us to sin, but if we do, Christ already paid the price for our sins. He will forgive us if we have godly sorrow and ask for forgiveness.

For a just man falleth seven times, and riseth up again: but the wicked shall fall into mischief. — Proverbs 24:16

If we confess our sins, he is faithful and just to forgive us our sins, and to cleanse us from all unrighteousness. — 1 John 1:9

I regret most of the sins that I willfully committed after I confessed Christ, which were many. I had accepted Jesus in 1992 and confessed Him as my Savior, but I did not fall in love with Him until I decided to let Him be Lord in my life. Honestly, I got saved because I knew that if I didn't, I would spend eternity in hell. Nonetheless, after years of being a hypocrite, going under the title of being a Christian, I truly fell in love with Him. Then I began to let Him lead and guide me daily. I could have avoided years of setbacks, setups, detours, heartache, hurts, pains, and shame. I fought shame and being upset with myself for allowing the enemy to fool me for so long. I was truly repentant. Therefore, I had to forgive and stop condemning myself because God had forgiven me. When God forgives, He does not remember our sins. Always be quick to repent.

There is therefore now no condemnation to them which are in Christ Jesus, who walk not after the flesh, but after the Spirit. — Romans 8:1

[18] Who is a God like unto thee, that pardoneth iniquity, and passeth by the transgression of the remnant of his heritage? he retaineth not his anger forever, because he delighteth in mercy.
[19] He will turn again, he will have compassion upon us; he will subdue our iniquities; and thou wilt cast all their sins into the depths of the sea. — Micah 7:18-19

With all the tactics and devices of the enemy, coupled with our sinful nature, we must be determined to live for God. We must be tenacious and relentless in our fight to live for God. It all comes when we make up in our minds that nothing and no one is worth our salvation. All the pleasures of the world are not worth us living lives that are displeasing to God, subsequently, losing our soul and spending eternity in hell.

SUMMARY

For some of us, labor pains on this journey to deliverance began at birth. After birth, we have no voice in how we are raised nor how our childhood will birth itself out. As children, we are at the mercy of our parents or of the ones that raise us. For some, a major part of our childhood, we may have felt hopeless, helpless, and unhappy. Some of us have very few fond memories of growing up. However, we must try and move past the pain, hurt, shame, and feeling of being rejected. Though this may not be true in every situation, there are times when the parents do the best they can with the tools they were given. Some parents imitate their parents and the way they were raised. Some parents were in a loving and caring home, while others may have come from an abusive and dysfunctional home. However, we should endeavor to learn from the mistakes that our parents made and strive not to make the same with our children.

Most likely, if one's childhood was not a loving one, counseling and deliverance are needed before and after reaching adulthood. All those old wounds need to be healed before we can forgive and move successfully into a healed, healthy, and happy adult. What's more? Inner healing and deliverance are needed to break ungodly soul ties that were formed with abusive and manipulative parents. Also, anger, bitterness, and unforgiveness towards our parents can be released through deliverance so everyone involved can move forward. Forgiveness is not necessarily for the abuser; it is for the one that felt abused. If the pains from our childhood are not properly addressed, they can affect our near and distant future. If we are not fully delivered, after being abused, we could unintentionally become an abuser. Furthermore, if we are not properly healed from our past, then we are prone to make unwise and detrimental choices in our lives.

For instance, if we lacked a loving and nurturing childhood, we may inadvertently search for unsafe ways to compensate and fill those voids. For me, I got involved with drugs, promiscuity, and found myself in several unhealthy and dangerous relationships with men. I lacked the knowledge about deliverance and inner healing when I reached adulthood. I would not find out until forty years later that the enemy was trying to derail my destiny and destroy me in the process. Even after I gave my life to the Lord, I was yet ignorant of the fact that I needed to be healed and delivered to be totally free to live a life free of guilt and shame. Just as the unhealthy soul ties that were formed with abusive parents needed to be broken, likewise, unhealthy soul ties with past sexual partners, manipulative spiritual leaders, or even with some friends also need to be broken through deliverance. Deliverance will close the doors to the enemy that were opened by being abused by others and oneself. If there is no deliverance in our lives, those opened doors remain open, and the enemy will have the legal right to attack. It's indeed possible to go through life, unaware that we have unsevered soul ties and wounds from the past that need to be healed through forgiving and accepting forgiveness in our lives.

The road to deliverance begins with accepting Christ as our personal Savior. Being born again and living a life that is pleasing unto Him is the wisest decision we could ever make in this life. Accepting salvation and being born again is only the beginning of this Christian journey. However, salvation alone does not automatically deliver us from entanglements nor some of the consequences that were bought about by negative choices or other unfavorable events from our past. After salvation, we must pray for the gift of the Holy Ghost. Even after receiving the Holy Ghost, we should be thankful, but not satisfied. We must pray for spiritual discernment for God to lead us to a deliverance ministry. The leaders need to walk in true holiness, have the heart of God, lead by example, preach and teach the Word of God, walk with spiritual power and authority, and genuinely care for their sheep. Since the Bible tells us that there are wolves in sheep's clothing, we must beware of false prophets and manipulative spiritual leaders. We must use spiritual discernment, study and know God's word, and don't allow ourselves to be dominated, manipulated, or controlled by any parent, spiritual leader, or by anyone. Likewise, if we find ourselves in an abusive marriage or romantic relationship, we should pray and let God lead us on how to leave that relationship safely.

It takes a special anointing and grace to labor with the people and help walk them through deliverance. Being planted in a God-centered ministry is vital to one's deliverance from the hurt, shame, rejection, unforgiveness, bitterness, and abuse from our pasts. A ministry strong in deliverance is crucial when there are ungodly soul ties, generational curses, and other demonic oppressions that need to be broken off people's lives. We should be tenacious and hungry for more than just a nice Sunday sermon. To be totally set free from the woes of our past, we need to be taught about spiritual warfare and how to fight in the spiritual realm. If we do not learn how to fight the enemy in the spirit, we could become a weak Christian and may possibly find ourselves backsliding to some of our past sins.

No one is perfect. We are bound to sin and make mistakes. But when we do, we should be quick to humble ourselves, repent to God, turn from sin, and accept Christ's forgiveness. We should always strive to keep a pure heart, forgive others, and keep the love for God and His people. We should become fully submitted to God, strive to grow in Him, and be happy and joy in our salvation. We should trust God, have faith in Him to do His will, hold onto Him no matter what, because He is faithful, and He won't fail us. We should never be ashamed to ask a discreet and mature believer to pray and stand with us in prayer for any weakness or any struggles that we may encounter. As always, be sure to be led and directed by God as to who to trust, and from whom to seek counsel. Even when it comes to a spiritual leader, follow them only as they follow Christ. If God let you discern that the spiritual leader is operating in the flesh and not by His Spirit, by no means follow them. Pray for God to lead you to a true man or woman of God for counsel and direction. Pray without ceasing and never stop praying for God's guidance.

Although I have experienced many labor pains to get to this place of deliverance that I have attained, this by no means exempts me from future trials and the need for future deliverance. I have by no means arrived, nor will I ever arrive at a place in God where I won't need His deliverance power in my life.

In Philippians 3:12-16, the Apostle Paul wrote: (MESSAGE)

12-14 I'm not saying that I have this all together, that I have it made. But I am well on my way, reaching out for Christ, who has so wondrously reached out for me. Friends don't get me wrong: By no means do I count myself an expert in all of this, but I've got my eye on the goal, where God is beckoning us onward—to Jesus. I'm off and running, and I'm not turning back.

15-16 So let's keep focused on that goal, those of us who want everything God has for us. If any of you have something else in mind, something less than total commitment, God will clear your blurred vision—you'll see it yet! Now that we're on the right track, let's stay on it.

Through all the trials and the afflictions that I have endured, I continue to press towards the mark. I keep my eyes fixed on Jesus, who is the author and the finisher of my faith. Even though sometimes I have felt like I had no more fight left in me, through prayer, I have endured and will continue to do so until the day of Jesus Christ. Every spiritual labor pain has birthed me into a new dimension in God. There will always be another trial and test. I pray without ceasing because God is, and He always will be, my Deliverer.

SUMMARY NUGGETS TO HELP BABES IN CHRIST AVOID UNECESSARY BIRTHING PANGS!

I've been through a lot of heartaches, hurt, and shame on this journey. I've not been ashamed because of what others thought, rather ashamed that I allowed myself to be dominated, manipulated, and controlled. Also, ashamed that I let the enemy deceive me into sin when I know that God always provides a way of escape from temptation. Then again, I have learned from every mistake and trial. These mistakes and trials have worked for my good in that after God delivered me, I developed a hunger and a thirst for righteousness. I came out more tenacious and determined to serve God. In addition, a spirit of compassion was birthed out of me that otherwise, I may not possess the degree that I do now. May I suggest some nuggets that I have learned over the past twenty plus years that may be of some assistance to someone that has a made-up mind to live for Christ. Had I been privy to these nuggets, I could have avoided so many snares of the enemy. I have found that some of the pains we endure on this Christian journey may not even be about us; it may be to help others.

- Accepting Christ as Lord and Savior in your heart is just the beginning. Accepting salvation can happen anywhere, not only in the physical church house.

- Pray to be filled with the Holy Ghost. Pray for God to lead you to the right ministry that is strong in deliverance. Surround yourself with other believers that are strong in prayer.

- All the gifts of the Holy Spirit are important and should be desired, but I feel that the gift of the discerning of spirits is especially vital to every person's early walk with God. There are many spirits, but only one Holy Spirit. The immature Christian can be easily deceived and misled by the wrong spirit if they do not have a discerning of spirits. Discerning of spirits will enable you to discern what and who is of God and what and who is not of God.

[1] Beloved, believe not every spirit, but try the spirits whether they are of God: because many false prophets are gone out into the world.
[2] Hereby know ye the Spirit of God: Every spirit that confesseth that Jesus Christ is come in the flesh is of God:
[3] And every spirit that confesseth not that Jesus Christ is come in the flesh is not of God: and this is that spirit of antichrist, whereof ye have heard that it should come; and even now already is it in the world. — 1 John 4:1-3

- I highly recommend that you find spiritual leadership and get planted in a church where there is a true prophet that is also a seer. Beware, because like the above Scriptures states, there are false prophets out there in the church as well. Because they are anointed does not automatically make them righteous. Check their fruits.

- After receiving the Holy Ghost, in-dept deliverance will probably be needed. For someone like myself that had been into drugs and sexual sins, those spirits may try to hide and lie dormant until a later time. When the enemy sees that a believer's guard is down and may have become weak and weary, then whatever was lying dormant will try to resurface. With sexual sins, ungodly soul ties were formed and will need to be severed by the power of the blood. In a good deliverance ministry, they will be able to walk you through the steps to get complete deliverance. Here is where a seer prophet is needed to be able to see in the spirit what may have attached itself to you and need to be uprooted. You will need to renounce some past alignments and ungodly soul ties, then fall out of agreement with them.

- Some past wounds may need to be healed. Healing can come in many forms, whether it's talking to someone that is discreet, or it may come through forgiving the people that hurt you.

- Do not hold onto bitterness and unforgiveness. It is a sin and holding onto it can cause sickness in one's body. If we don't forgive others, God won't forgive us. Matthew 6:15 says, "But if ye forgive not men their trespasses, neither will your Father forgive your trespasses." Thus, we must forgive others, no matter how they may have hurt us. Be quick to forgive. It frees you from being tied to that person that hurt you.

- Stay close to God by fasting, praying, and reading your Bible. Stay hungry for more of God, never become satisfied. Always keep the fear of God. Proverbs 9:10 states that the fear of the Lord is the beginning of wisdom.

If you feel yourself getting weak and tempted by the enemy, quickly pray for God to lead you to someone that is stronger than yourself and get them to pray for you and with you. Get them to agree with you in prayer. There is power in agreement. Don't be shy to ask for help. The enemy will surely come and try to seduce you in some way or another. Therefore, fight with everything within you to not give in to temptation. James 4:7 lets us know that if we "submit yourselves therefore to God. Resist the devil, and he will flee from you." If you willingly submit and give into sin, sinning then becomes easier, thus harder to break away from.

- When it comes to spiritual leadership, it's good to have a pastor/leader that is after the heart of God and one that directs you to God and not to themselves. But however, there are some that are not after the heart of God. Therefore, always rely on the Holy Spirit and use your discernment. Whatever God shows you, believe that. It does not matter if a person is an apostle, a prophet, an evangelistic, a pastor, or a teacher. If God shows you their heart and aim, and if it is not righteous or according to the Word of God, trust the Holy Spirit and act accordingly. It does not matter if a person says, "God says," if your spirit does not bear witness with what they are saying and if it is not biblical, always follow the leading of the Holy Spirit. This is so very important. If I had acted according to my discernment, I would have saved myself a lot of hurt from spiritual leadership.

- Always judge prophecy. If you get a check in your spirit that the words spoken to you by whoever is not of God, don't receive it into your spirit. Rebuke it, and you won't have to wage warfare over it later.

- No one is perfect. The Bible tells us in Proverbs that a just man will fall seven times, but he will rise again. Consequently, we are bound to make mistakes, and when we do, we should quickly humble ourselves, repent to God and get back in the race.

- Keep a pure heart, love God and His word. Love the truth and know that God is the only righteous judge.

THE END

ABOUT THE AUTHOR

Beverly Barnes Brown accepted the call of God on her life twenty-eight years ago. Beverly Barnes Brown is called and anointed in prayer and intercession. She is a first-time author that has a passion for the hurting and lost souls.

Beverly began working at plywood plants to support her daughters. Knowing that God had something better and greater for her, she applied and was accepted into college. She received an Associates degree in Computer Programming from Angelina College in 1997. Shortly after receiving that degree, her focus shifted to the prison ministry. She began to minister to convicted offenders as a correctional officer, where she worked on the Texas Death Row for ten years. Beverly worked as a church secretary for over twenty years. She also worked with the deliverance team in ministry.

After leaving the prison ministry, she enrolled again into Angelina College into a nursing program. Beverly became a licensed vocational nurse in 2013. She worked private duty nursing for a few years before deciding to work with the elderly community at Memory Care facilities. She loves caring for the elderly with Dementia issues.

Beverly also holds certificates in Biblical Studies. She has attended many conferences and has taken numerous classes in spiritual warfare and deliverance. She has read and continues to study numerous books by trusted and well know authors concerning warfare, prayer, and deliverance. The best training to date is the teaching of the Holy Spirit through the things that she has suffered and overcame. She loves God with all her heart and endeavors to please Him with the anointing that He has entrusted her with. She is uniquely graced to labor and toil with God's people until strongholds in their lives are pulled down and they walk in total victory. Beverly is in full time ministry and holds prayer gatherings frequently. She prays and teaches via social media. She can be contacted through her Facebook ministry page, Beverly Brown. She is the mother of two beautiful daughters and resides in the Dallas-Forth area in Texas.

INDEX

A

abomination, 87–88, 110
abortion, 20
abuser, 13, 46, 138–39
adultery, 50–51, 133
affair, 13–14, 16, 31, 43, 47, 78–79
afflictions, 2, 131–34, 142
AIDS, 19, 22–23
angels, 12, 49, 135
anger, 8, 108, 122–23, 136, 138
anointing, 92–93, 149
apostles, 38, 58, 84, 95, 100–101, 146
arrogance, 67, 125
atmosphere, 25, 64, 85, 99
attention, 71, 86–87
authority, 3, 51, 71, 117, 127, 140

B

backslidden, 43
baptism, 26, 39, 69
battles, 2, 49–50, 63, 72
believers, 53, 59, 65, 69, 78, 108, 110, 126, 144
Bible, 14, 20, 31, 55–56, 65–66, 69, 80, 101, 113, 115, 125, 128, 131, 140, 145–46
birth, 2–3, 13, 138
birth canal, 52–53
bitterness, 57, 122, 128, 138, 140, 145

bless, 64, 67, 102, 124
blessings, 85, 87–88, 97, 105–6, 110–11, 115, 123
blood, 2, 41–42, 49, 71, 74–75, 85–86, 88, 112, 126, 133–34, 145
bloodline, 116–17
bondage, 2–3, 10, 18, 92, 117

C

cardinal sins, 43
charismatic witchcraft, 56–58, 69, 71, 118, 132
Charlotte, 110, 113, 116, 119, 126, 129–30
church services, 24, 60, 79–80, 98, 120
compassion, 4, 50, 136, 143
compromise, 74, 77, 81, 95, 108–9
condemnation, 72, 78, 136
conferences, 99, 107, 121, 124, 148
confusion, 34–35, 57, 122
contrite spirit, 37, 82
control, 2, 8, 25, 27, 54, 56–60, 64, 69, 132–33
countenance, 36, 38
covenant, 42, 118–19, 124
covetous, 76, 78, 93–94
curses, 64, 87–89, 117

D

darkness, 2–3, 49, 71, 74, 86, 88, 97
deaths, 41, 72, 75, 83, 96, 110
degree, 143, 148
deliverance, 2–3, 38–40, 47–48, 50–51, 70, 73, 103–6, 115, 117, 119–23, 125, 127–28, 131–34, 138–41, 148
deliverance ministry, 76, 107, 140
demonic attacks, 2, 87, 114, 120, 127

demons, 50, 86, 93, 112
destiny, 2, 100, 112, 139
destruction, 52, 107
devil, 48–49, 52, 56, 59, 78–79, 86, 95, 111, 114, 128, 135, 146
diligent, 36, 53, 72
discern, 103, 120–21, 123, 126, 141, 144
discernment, 33, 76, 84, 90, 103, 127, 146
discreet, 50, 141, 145
disease, 23
dreams, 90, 117–19
drugs, 9, 17–21, 27, 29, 31, 37–38, 40, 43, 50–51, 71, 110, 132, 139, 144

E

evangelists, 24, 100
evil, 15, 19, 52, 55, 60, 87, 96, 110, 125, 129, 131–32
evil spirits, 2, 86, 120

F

faint, 81, 126, 128
faith, 2, 70, 74, 76–77, 86, 91, 103–5, 112, 126, 141–42
false prophets, 107–8, 144
fear, 7–8, 15, 20, 22–23, 53, 58, 83, 88, 91, 95, 98, 100, 125–26, 145
fear of God, 83, 93–94, 145
flesh, 2, 41, 46, 49, 63, 71–72, 86, 133, 136, 141, 144
forgiveness, 32, 41, 43, 67, 70, 72, 122, 124, 134, 136, 138–39
freedom, 10–11, 92
fruits, 53, 55, 103, 105, 108, 111, 144

G

gates, 5, 52, 107
gifts, 26, 32–33, 69–70, 101, 112, 140, 144
glory, 5–6, 15, 28, 34, 54–55, 73, 76, 79, 81–82, 98–99, 105, 117–18, 123, 127, 135
godliness, 76
gospel, 61, 86, 92, 94, 97, 135
grace, 19, 21, 25, 42, 44, 50, 77, 94, 108, 124, 132, 140
guidance, 36, 56, 141

H

harvest, 121
health, 61
heart, 18, 20, 22, 28, 30, 34–38, 40, 49–50, 66–67, 73, 77–78, 81–82, 124, 134–35, 146
heaven, 5–6, 24, 28, 44, 60–61, 73, 82–83, 105, 120, 123, 130, 134–35
hell, 5–6, 84, 97, 135–37
HIV, 19
holy, 34, 45, 53, 81, 109
Holy Ghost, 24–28, 35, 38–39, 44, 46, 48, 50, 66, 73, 81–82, 90, 95, 113, 140, 144
Holy Spirit, 27–28, 30, 47–48, 51, 69, 71–72, 127, 144, 146, 148
homosexuality, 110
humble, 44, 60, 76, 81
humility, 32, 81

I

Idolatry, 133
ignorance, 51, 71–72
incubus spirit, 120–21
infirmities, 74, 113

iniquities, 50, 54, 75, 89, 134, 136
intercession, 80, 83–85, 96, 148
intimacy, 45–46
intimate relationship, 6, 28, 35, 79

J

jealous, 11–12
Jesus, 2, 19, 26, 39, 69, 76, 86, 88, 96, 112, 119, 123, 126, 133–34, 141–42
joy, 3–4, 12, 21, 27–28, 45, 56, 106, 131, 141
judgment, 15, 42, 45, 67, 94, 96, 108

K

kingdom, 6, 27, 46, 77, 86, 133
knowledge, 19, 23, 41, 54–55, 70, 75–76, 87–89, 96, 107, 133, 139

L

labor pains, 131, 138, 141
law, 42, 54, 72, 89
life, 4–5, 7–12, 17, 19–23, 25–31, 34–36, 38–40, 49–52, 69–70, 72–73, 75, 92–94, 131–32, 135–36, 139
locusts, 60–61
love, 4, 10–11, 14, 31–32, 67, 76–77, 83, 97–98, 105, 108, 122, 124, 131, 136, 140
lust, 43, 70, 77

M

manifestation, 60, 70, 111–12, 131
manipulation, 49, 56, 63–64, 66–67, 69, 132–33

marriage, 2, 13–14, 16–17, 29, 105, 132
masturbation, 50
mercy, 15, 19, 42, 45, 68, 83, 89, 136, 138
Merlendi, 83–85, 87, 98–99, 102–5, 107–10, 112–13, 119–23, 126–28
mighty, 26, 42, 49, 62–63
ministry, 38, 47–48, 51, 58, 62, 64, 66–68, 82, 99–100, 102, 106–8, 118–19, 122–24, 140, 148
miracles, 59, 70, 95–96, 128
miracle worker, 93
money, 18, 21, 65–66, 77, 99, 115, 118
murders, 96, 110, 133

O

obedience, 49, 63
obstruction, 49, 63
offense, 123–25
offerings, 65, 102, 111, 119, 124

P

passion, 15, 31, 96, 148
peace, 3–4, 14, 19, 21–22, 27–29, 31, 61, 67, 81, 86, 104–5, 122, 127, 129, 131
perseverance, 3–4, 82
power, 26–28, 30, 32, 58–59, 71, 76, 82–83, 86, 88, 92, 95, 97, 126–27, 133–35, 145
pray, 6, 25–26, 47–50, 60–61, 66, 68–69, 80–87, 89–91, 93, 106, 110, 112–13, 118–24, 140–42, 144–45
prayer CD, 122, 124
prayer warriors, 25–26, 47, 50, 68, 81–82, 85

praying, 6, 20, 31, 40, 60–61, 70–71, 80, 82, 87–89, 91, 102, 112, 118–19, 124, 130
pregnancy, 13, 20–21
pride, 4, 56, 67, 78, 95, 125
priests, 54–55, 62, 83
principalities, 2, 49, 71, 86
profit, 19, 104
promises, 41, 110–11
prophecy, 70, 100–102, 108, 111–12, 117
prophesy, 100–101, 117
prophetic, 86, 88, 99–100, 106
prophetic word, 25, 100–101, 104, 107–8, 110–12
prophets, 24–25, 54, 99–101, 107, 116–24, 144, 146
provisions, 44, 72

R

rebuke, 48, 51, 77, 85–86, 96, 111–12, 127, 146
rejection, 5, 125, 140
religion, 33, 35–36, 45, 77, 79
repent, 26, 44, 48, 62, 67, 69, 71–73, 93–94, 98, 134–36, 140, 146
repentance, 3, 51, 60–62, 94, 98, 134
repentant, 26, 32, 44, 47, 72, 136
reprobate mind, 96
resistance, 36, 51
revelation, 5–6, 50, 52, 55, 68, 73, 81, 98, 112, 127
revenge, 13–14, 63, 125
revival, 23–24, 59–60, 79, 84, 95, 110
revivalists, 96–97
righteous, 2, 22, 44, 82, 131, 144, 146
righteousness, 9, 15, 27, 34–35, 59, 86, 95, 130, 135, 143

S

sacrifice, 22, 41–42, 45, 60–61, 82, 85, 92, 128
safety, 19, 127
salvation, 15, 28, 32–33, 35–37, 50, 53, 69–71, 73–74, 80, 84, 86, 134–35, 137, 139–41, 143
seer, 118, 144
selling drugs, 17, 21, 31
sex, 12, 19, 41, 43, 46, 55
  unprotected, 10, 19, 23
shame, 43, 54–55, 57, 72, 106, 123, 132, 136, 138–40, 143
shepherds, 53, 55, 57, 76, 93, 123, 125
sinful, 41
sins, 26, 28, 31, 33, 41–48, 53–55, 57–58, 60–62, 70–76, 93, 95–97, 109–10, 133–36, 140, 145–46
   sexual, 41, 46–47, 144–45
smoking, 18, 21–22, 40
social media, 85, 99, 107, 122, 124, 149
souls, 6, 15, 19, 22, 24–26, 45, 50–51, 56, 59, 74–75, 78–80, 83–85, 90, 94, 96–97
soul ties, 3, 38, 41, 47, 49, 57–58, 69–71, 138, 140, 145
sow, 65, 68, 103
spiritual leaders, 54, 62, 64, 77, 81, 108, 123, 132–33, 140–41
spiritual warfare, 50–51, 58, 68, 71, 85–87, 99, 120, 127, 140, 148
strength, 3, 22, 28, 31, 47–50, 65, 71, 73–74, 86, 113, 119–20, 127, 130
strongholds, 43, 47, 49–51, 62, 67–68, 73, 99, 149
stumble, 54, 125

T

tarrying, 25
temptation, 40–41, 43–44, 143, 146
testimony, 127, 129

Texas, 15, 101–2, 109–10, 112, 115–17, 126, 128, 149
thorns, 55, 103, 108
tithes, 45, 66–67, 102, 111, 124
tongues, 9, 25, 41, 69–70, 113
transgressions, 89, 136
transition, 35, 112
trials, 19, 30, 141–43
tribulations, 30
trust, 2, 57, 109, 129, 131, 141, 146
trusting, 103, 129
truth, 11, 41–42, 53, 76–77, 86, 89, 91, 109, 117, 147
turmoil, 8, 61

U

unforgiveness, 37, 40, 122, 124, 138, 140, 145
unhappiness, 13
unrighteous, 46

V

vengeance, 14, 42, 125, 135
vigilant, 78, 128
vision, 5, 90
vulnerability, 57

W

war, 63
warfare, 49–50, 63, 71–72, 127, 148
weaknesses, 39, 43, 141
weapons, 9, 49, 63
wickedness, 75, 96

wisdom, 33, 37, 70, 89, 145
witchcraft, 56–57, **88**, 133
witnesses, 28, 42, 146
word of God, 5–6, 33–34, 40, 53, 66, 86, 91, 94–95, 101, 111, 140, 146
worship, 61, 116, 123, 130
wrath, 14, 125, 133, 135

Z

zeal, 33, 56

www.ingramcontent.com/pod-product-compliance
Lightning Source LLC
Chambersburg PA
CBHW072014110526
44592CB00012B/1300